CONDUCTI

CLASSIC

GROUNDED

THEORY

for BUSINESS *and* MANAGEMENT STUDENTS

Sara Miller McCune founded SAGE Publishing in 1965 to support the dissemination of usable knowledge and educate a global community. SAGE publishes more than 1000 journals and over 800 new books each year, spanning a wide range of subject areas. Our growing selection of library products includes archives, data, case studies and video. SAGE remains majority owned by our founder and after her lifetime will become owned by a charitable trust that secures the company's continued independence.

Los Angeles | London | New Delhi | Singapore | Washington DC | Melbourne

CONDUCTING CLASSIC GROUNDED THEORY

for BUSINESS and MANAGEMENT STUDENTS

ISABELLE WALSH, JUDITH A. HOLTON & GAËTAN MOURMANT

$SAGE

Los Angeles | London | New Delhi
Singapore | Washington DC | Melbourne

Los Angeles | London | New Delhi
Singapore | Washington DC | Melbourne

SAGE Publications Ltd
1 Oliver's Yard
55 City Road
London EC1Y 1SP

SAGE Publications Inc.
2455 Teller Road
Thousand Oaks, California 91320

SAGE Publications India Pvt Ltd
B 1/I 1 Mohan Cooperative Industrial Area
Mathura Road
New Delhi 110 044

SAGE Publications Asia-Pacific Pte Ltd
3 Church Street
#10-04 Samsung Hub
Singapore 049483

Editor: Ruth Stitt
Assistant editor: Martha Cunneen
Production editor: Sarah Cooke
Marketing manager: Lucia Sweet
Cover design: Francis Kenney
Typeset by: C&M Digitals (P) Ltd, Chennai, India
Printed in the UK

Library of Congress Control Number: 2019938031

British Library Cataloguing in Publication data

A catalogue record for this book is available from
the British Library

ISBN 978-1-5264-6007-3
ISBN 978-1-5264-6008-0 (pbk)

At SAGE we take sustainability seriously. Most of our products are printed in the UK using responsibly sourced
papers and boards. When we print overseas we ensure sustainable papers are used as measured by the PREPS
grading system. We undertake an annual audit to monitor our sustainability.

CONTENTS

LIST OF FIGURES AND TABLES

FIGURES

TABLES

EDITORS' INTRODUCTION TO THE *MASTERING BUSINESS RESEARCH METHODS* SERIES

Welcome to the *Mastering Business Research Methods* series. In recent years, there has been a great increase in the numbers of students reading for master's level degrees across the business and management disciplines. A considerable number of these students are expected to prepare a dissertation towards the end of their degree programme in a timeframe of three to four months. For many this takes place after their taught modules have finished and is expected to be an independent piece of work. Whilst each student is supported in their dissertation or research project by an academic supervisor, they will need to find out more detailed information about the method that they intend to use. Before starting dissertations or research projects, students have usually been provided with little more than an overview of a wide range of methods in preparation for what is often daunting task. If you are one such student, you are not alone. As university professors with a deep interest in research methods, we have provided this series of books to help people like you. Each book gives detailed information about a particular method, approach or task to support you in your dissertation. We understand both what is involved in master's level dissertations and what help students need to understand research methods in order to excel when writing a dissertation. This series is the only one that is designed with the specific objective of helping master's level students to prepare their dissertations.

Most books in our series are dedicated to either a method of data collection or a method of data analysis. They are intended to be read by you when undertaking the particular stage of the research process - of either data collection or analysis - and they are designed to provide sufficient knowledge for you to complete that stage. There are some other books, such as those on *Mixed Methods* or *Action Research*, where the nature of the approach means that one method is inextricably linked with others. Those books are designed to provide you with a comprehensive understanding of the approach, although it may be necessary to supplement your reading of one or other of these books by reading another book on a particular method that you intend to employ when utilizing that approach. All books in the series are written in a clear way by highly respected authors who have considerable experience of teaching and writing about research methods. To help you find your way around each one, we have utilized a standard format. That is to say that each book is organized into six chapters:

- **Chapter 1** introduces the method, considers how the method emerged for what purposes, and provides an outline of the remainder of the book.
- **Chapter 2** addresses the underlying philosophical assumptions that inform the uses of particular methods.
- **Chapter 3** discusses the components of the relevant method.
- **Chapter 4** considers the way in which the different components may be organized to use the method.
- **Chapter 5** provides examples of published studies that have used the method.
- **Chapter 6** concludes by reflecting on the strengths and weaknesses of that method.

We hope that reading your chosen books helps you in your dissertation.

Bill Lee, Mark NK Saunders and VK Narayanan

ABOUT THE SERIES EDITORS

Bill Lee, PhD is Professor of Accounting at the University of Sheffield, UK. He has a long-standing interest in research methods and practice, in addition to his research into accounting and accountability issues. Bill's research has been published widely, including in: *Accounting Forum*; *British Accounting Review*; *Critical Perspectives on Accounting*; *Journal of Applied Behavioral Science*; *Management Accounting Research*; *Omega*; *Organization Studies*; and *Work, Employment & Society*. His publications in the area of research methods and practice include the co-edited collections *The Real Life Guide to Accounting Research* and *Challenges and Controversies in Management Research*.

Mark NK Saunders, BA MSc PGCE PhD FCIPD is Professor of Business Research Methods and Director of PhD Programmes at Birmingham Business School, University of Birmingham, UK. His research interests are research methods, in particular methods for participant selection and for understanding intra organizational relationships; human resource aspects of the management of change, in particular trust within and between organizations; and small and medium-sized enterprises. Mark's research has been published in journals including: *British Journal of Management*; *Journal of Small Business Management*; *Field Methods*; *Human Relations*; *Management Learning*; and *R&D Management, Social Science and Medicine*. He has co-authored and co-edited a range of books including *Research Methods for Business Students* (currently in its seventh edition) and the *Handbook of Research Methods on Trust* (currently in its second edition).

VK Narayanan is the Deloitte Touché Stubbs Professor of Strategy and Entrepreneurship in Le Bow College of Business, Drexel University, Philadelphia, PA. His articles have appeared in leading professional journals such as: *Academy of Management Journal*; *Academy of Management Review*; *Accounting Organizations and Society*; *Journal of Applied Psychology*; *Journal of Management*; *Journal of Management*

Studies; Management Information Systems Quarterly; R&D Management; and *Strategic Management Journal.* He has authored or co-authored several books, including *Managing Technology and Innovation for Competitive Advantage,* and has co-edited the *Encyclopaedia of Technology and Innovation Management.*

ABOUT THE AUTHORS

Isabelle Walsh is Distinguished Professor of Management and, currently, Associate Dean of the Digitalization Academy at Skema Business School, Université Côte d'Azur, France. During her career, she has managed several research groups, master's and doctoral programs. Beside methodological and research design issues (which include classic grounded theory with mixed data and bibliometrics), her research interests include Information Systems usage, strategic alignment, quality in higher education, knowledge sharing, and cultural and change management issues. Her research has been published in several international top-tier outlets: *European Journal of Information Systems*; *Journal of Strategic Information Systems*; *Organizational Research Methods*; *Systèmes d'Information & Management*, *The Grounded Theory Review* amongst others. Most of her published empirical research adopts a grounded theory approach with mixed qualitative and quantitative data. Her teaching is aligned with her research interests. Beyond her academic achievements, she has extensive corporate and consultancy experience.

Judith A. Holton is Associate Professor of Management at Mount Allison University, Canada, where she teaches strategy, leadership, and organizational change. She completed her master's in Leadership at Royal Roads University, Victoria (Canada), and her PhD in Management Studies at the University of Northampton (UK). During her PhD research, she was closely mentored by Barney Glaser. She has written a number of methodological papers and co-edited books about classic grounded theory, and was the founding editor of *The Grounded Theory Review* as a peer-reviewed journal dedicated to classic grounded theory research. In addition to research methodology, her research interests include leadership and management of complex systems, organizational change, learning and innovation in knowledge work. She has published in: *Organizational Research Methods*; *Management Learning*; *The Learning Organization*; *Leadership and Organization Development Journal*; *Advances in Developing Human Resources*; and *The Grounded Theory Review*. She is co-author, with Isabelle Walsh, of *Classic Grounded Theory: Applications with Qualitative and Quantitative Data.*

Gaëtan Mourmant has a dual PhD degree in Management Information Systems from Paris Dauphine University and Georgia State University. Gaëtan is the founder of a successful company in the domain of e-learning and data analysis. He is also a visiting professor at Iéseg School of Management and Business Science Institute. Gaëtan also taught at Georgia State University and Paris Dauphine, and was also assistant professor at EM Strasbourg. His research interests are related to entrepreneurial decision-making and classic grounded theory. He has published papers in: the *European Journal of Information Systems; DATABASE for Advances in Information Systems; Journal of Management, Spirituality & Religion; International Conference for Information Systems; ACM-SIGMIS CPR Conference;* as well as *The Grounded Theory Review.* Gaëtan is the founder of www.DoingGT.com, a website dedicated to the study of grounded theory.

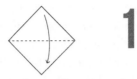

1

AN INTRODUCTION TO GROUNDED THEORY

'This license [to discover and generate new theories] is a "eureka" type joy and an obvious good opportunity to make a contribution to a substantive field. Some still cannot believe they are allowed this right and power. It is academic freedom to the max.' (Glaser, 1998: 133)

INTRODUCTION

You may approach your research in many different ways, using different data-collection methods and analysis techniques. Although classic grounded theory (GT: see Glaser & Strauss, 1967; Glaser, 1978; Holton & Walsh, 2017) welcomes many different data-collection methods, it provides a precise and comprehensive set of systematic procedures to sample and analyze data. In this chapter, after briefly explaining the different ways through which you may approach your research (deductive, inductive and/or abductive), we answer what we consider a fundamental question related to the GT approach (whether it is strictly limited to qualitative research or if it welcomes any type of data, qualitative and/or quantitative), and we highlight its different streams (classic or Glaserian, Straussian, etc.), to allow you to decide for yourself if GT is suited to your research purpose.

To avoid possible misunderstandings, in this introduction we define some words commonly used by many authors with different meanings. We do not claim that these definitions are valid across all domains for all authors, however, they will apply throughout the chapters that follow. Therefore **data-collection methods** for example are the media through which data are collected in a research project, e.g. interviews, observation, filming or surveys. The **analysis techniques** are the instruments used in a research project to help analyze and make sense of the collected data, e.g. text analysis, cluster analysis or structural equation modeling. The **methodology** is the specific combination of data-collection methods and analysis techniques used in a research project. The **framework** is the general set of guidelines proposed by some authors that you might choose to follow in a given project, e.g. those of Baskerville and Pries-Heje (1999) for action research, or those of Eisenhardt (1989) for case-study research. The **paradigm** is the worldview, which includes the philosophical assumptions that traditionally impact your ontological (i.e. what you consider does exist), epistemological (i.e. what you consider knowledge is), methodological (i.e. what set of data-collection methods/analysis techniques you consider may be used to obtain knowledge), and axiological (i.e. what you consider is valuable) beliefs/choices.

DIFFERENT WAYS TO APPROACH RESEARCH

When you conduct research in a given domain, broadly speaking, you can go about it in two general ways: a confirmatory hypothetico-deductive or exploratory inductive approach (see Figure 1.1).

You can start from one existing general theory that has been previously verified by other researchers as valid and test its hypotheses in a specific area and with a population that interests you. You can also use existing theories and knowledge to lay down some new hypotheses. You then collect data to verify these hypotheses. For example, you could use quantitative data through a survey with a statistically valid sample of the targeted population. This approach is *confirmatory hypothetico-deductive*, i.e. you confirm (or reject) hypotheses that you extracted or developed, based on existing theories discovered by other researchers and published in the existing literature. In other words, you deduce a theory from existing ones.

Alternatively, you can start with some qualitative and/or quantitative data, to investigate your domain of interest and explore the collected data to lay down some propositions (a statement that deals with new concepts or some elements, for which no measure has yet been developed) or hypotheses (a statement that deals with elements that may be measured, and that may be tested) towards perhaps what could be a totally new theory, which might be subsequently verified. This last approach is an *exploratory inductive approach* that is based on the exploration of your data, from which you propose a theory. You start with data collected from a specific population in a specific context and you infer a theory that may be more or less generalizable. In other words, you start with data and propose a theory that fits your data. This second option does not mean that you will ignore existing theories. It only means that you will investigate the literature and existing theories once your own theory has started to emerge. In some instances, you might eventually find new concepts or theories, enrich existing theories with new properties or dimensions, or you may find that you have confirmed an existing theory, which is also an interesting result in itself.

These two different research approaches are summarized in Figure 1.1. Examples of the two approaches to investigate the same research domain are provided in Box 1.1.

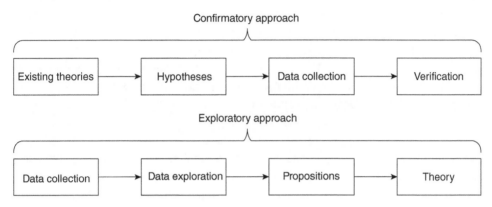

Figure 1.1   Different research approaches

Box 1.1   Examples of the two different basic approaches to conduct research

John and Mary have decided to do their respective master's projects in the domain of acceptance and use of new information technologies (IT); more particularly, they wish to investigate the different ways through which people approach and use new information technologies.

John chooses to use existing theories and adopt a confirmatory hypothetico-deductive approach. First, he investigates the literature and identifies the Technology Acceptance Model (TAM) as the model that is most often applied and validated in relation to IT acceptance and usage. The TAM tells him that the easier to use and the more useful a new IT is perceived, the more people will be intent on using it. John then lays down the hypothesis that if new virtual reality (VR) or augmented reality (AR) applications are perceived as useful and easy to use, people will be intent on using them. He collects quantitative data through a survey and tests if his hypothesis is verified in a statistically representative sample of his targeted population.

(Continued)

(Continued)

Mary wishes to adopt an exploratory approach to investigate what motivates people to use some new IT, without considering the TAM: she does not know anything about this model. She samples a population of very different people in terms of age, position, education, etc., with very different degrees of exposure to new IT. She does not lay down any hypothesis and remains in an exploratory inductive stance. She discovers that the more exposed and acculturated people are to technologies, the more they will be inclined to use any new virtual reality (VR) or augmented reality (AR) application proposed to them, irrelevant of their ease of use or usefulness. This result tends to contradict or complement TAM, a model that she will discover when she investigates the literature after she has laid down her own theoretical propositions.

We cannot talk about induction and deduction without at least mentioning abduction as a logic that complements induction and deduction towards eliminating or clarifying doubtful and/or unclear ideas: 'Deduction proves that something must be', 'induction shows that something actually is operative', while abduction suggests that 'something may be' (Peirce, 1965: §171) and is most probable. Box 1.2 below illustrates the logic of abduction as conceptualized by Peirce (you may find other conceptualizations of abduction, which are beyond the present book).

Box 1.2   Example of the logic of abduction

In the example of Mary's research above, Mary found that overall, in her sampled population, many of the younger people who were immersed in IT from a very young age, tended to be more IT acculturated and at ease with technologies than older people. She used qualitative data and her sample was not statistically valid. Hence, she could not deduct that age was an explanatory variable to IT acculturation. Using abductive logic, she inferred simply that age was a significant variable to take into account in her research. She decided to make sure to keep track of this demographic element for all participants as it might help explain IT acculturation.

This book is about an approach, a research process that helps to conduct research using the second option (exploratory inductive approach). We explore data to propose theories that may confirm, enrich or contradict existing ones. However, it has to be mentioned that even though doing GT is an overall exploratory inductive approach, it does use deductive and abductive reasoning in its research process (Glaser, 1978;

Walsh et al., 2015b). For instance, and as highlighted by Glaser (1978), the theoretical sampling that we will see in detail in Chapter 3 is deductive: you deduce where to sample next, based on an inducted hypothesis.

The GT research process allows the systematic generation of theory from data that have themselves been systematically obtained (Glaser, 1978). We must highlight that the term 'grounded theory' may itself lead you to some misunderstanding because it describes at the same time both the research process and the end result, i.e. a new theory that is empirically grounded in data. In the present book, and in order to clarify this issue, we use the abbreviation 'GT' when we mean the research process, the GT methodology; and we use the full term 'grounded theory' when we mean the end result of a GT study, i.e. a theory grounded in data. We must also highlight that classic GT may be considered at the same time as a data-collection method, an analysis technique, a methodology, a framework, a paradigm or an approach (Walsh et al., 2015a). In this book, we will use in the different chapters the term that best applies depending on the issue that is being debated.

In GT, the **main concern** is the prime motivator, interest or problem investigated. The result of GT, a grounded theory, is a conceptualized explanation of how the main concern is managed or resolved by those involved, i.e. the population investigated. For example, Holton (2007) investigates knowledge workers (professionals – doctors, nurses, professors, systems analysts, managers, consultants, etc. working in knowledge-based organizations) whose main concern emerges as being the dehumanizing impact of persistent and unpredictable change in their workplaces. In the examples provided in Box 1.1, the main concern that is being investigated could be 'understanding what makes people intent on using a new IT.'

A grounded theory is more than a description of research findings; it offers a theoretical explanation that is conceptually abstract and that is found to occur in diverse groups with a common concern (Glaser, 2003). GT focuses on participants' perspectives and provides them with opportunities to articulate their thoughts about issues they consider important, allowing them to reflect on these issues of concern. GT enables you to get close to the phenomenon under study, and participants' main concern, through extensive and iterative data collection and analysis, responding to latent patterns of social behavior as they emerge from the data and, through their conceptualization, serving as a guide for successive data collection and analyses. Conceptualizing data – simply put, 'naming a pattern' found as recurring in data – grounded in reality provides a powerful means both for understanding the world 'out there' and for developing action strategies that will allow some measure of control over it (Glaser & Strauss, 1967).

Concepts are abstract or generic ideas generalized from particular instances (*Merriam-Webster's* dictionary) within the data. Conceptualization is not an act of interpretation, it is an act of abstraction. This abstraction to a conceptual level explains theoretically rather than describes behavior that occurs in many diverse groups with a same concern (Glaser, 2003). GT's particular value is in this ability to provide a conceptual overview of the phenomenon under study – what is actually going on. As a research strategy, GT is particularly appropriate for studies of emerging organizational phenomena and complex environments. As the process of conceptualization is a rather abstract process, we provide two concrete illustrations of it in Box 1.3 below.

Box 1.3   Two illustrations of conceptualization

In these two illustrations, we show how a concept emerges from different accounts.

Letitia is exploring the subject of quality in higher education as perceived by the various stakeholders. She has interviewed students and professors in several universities, and has also used texts provided by accreditation bodies as sources of data. From the verbatims and text extracts like those below, she conceptualized the category 'Wanting reputation to be tangible' as being a significant expectation in relation to quality in higher education. *Source*: Loyola de Oliveira, work in progress, PhD Dissertation.

> 'The quality of the learning experience goes beyond the courses themselves that are being taught. You have to have adequate infrastructure: campus, classrooms, technology, etc.' (Professor)

> 'Sometimes, there are not enough seats in the classrooms. If we don't find extra chairs, some people have to sit on the floor or remain standing up.' (Student)

> 'The school's infrastructure fits its activities, e.g. campus-based learning, distance learning, research, and executive education. Classrooms, offices, laboratories, communications, and computer equipment, and other basic facilities are adequate for high-quality operations.' (Accreditation body: AACSB)

Miriam has conducted interviews in different firms to investigate pleasure and well-being at work. She asked people to describe their jobs, what they liked and disliked about them. From the collected verbatims like those below, she conceptualized the category 'Social ties' as having an important role in helping employees achieve well-being at work. *Source*: Schmidkontz, 2017, defended DBA dissertation

> 'I like being in contact with people. In my job, I have to work with many colleagues from different parts of the firm. Sometimes it is a lot but it is also why I like my job.' (Female, 45 years old)

> 'I don't see myself in this job in ten years but the main thing for me is the colleagues and the atmosphere.' (Female, 27 years old)

If we use a tree **metaphor**, the GT process could be seen as a tree whose roots are grounded in data (qualitative and/or quantitative data or any type of data), and the trunk and branches grow through the coding of the data. The fruits of the tree are grounded theories, knowing that the same set of data can lead to different theories (see Figure 1.2). However, one GT study usually proposes only one theory and different GT studies can be conducted using the same set of data, leading to several grounded theories.

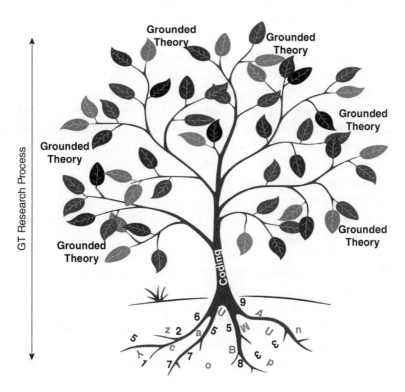

Figure 1.2   The GT tree - theories grounded in data

Throughout this book, as a means of simplification and to ease understanding, we will be using this tree metaphor to provide readers with a simple, global and integrated picture of the elements and issues discussed in different chapters.

IS GT A QUALITATIVE RESEARCH METHODOLOGY?

GT finds its sources in sociologist Barney Glaser's (1961) PhD dissertation, which he developed using only quantitative data. However, numbers cannot always tell a full story and you sometimes need qualitative data. This was the case for the famous

Awareness of Dying study written in 1965 by Glaser and another famous sociologist, Anselm Strauss. They conducted this study to understand the process of dying in hospitals; they used qualitative data exclusively, probably because quantitative data are insufficient when studying the social process through which 'living' patients in hospitals become 'dying' patients. The results of this study were so significant in the domain of nursing, that many people who read it and used its results asked the authors for details about the research methodology that they had applied to obtain such results. Therefore, Glaser and Strauss subsequently described their research methodology (GT) for this study in their seminal book *The Discovery of Grounded Theory* (Glaser & Strauss, 1967).

While the research approach proposed by Glaser and Strauss (1967) allows the use of both qualitative and/or quantitative data, it has been used primarily for qualitative studies because, at the time this approach was first developed, exploratory qualitative research was not well regarded in sociological circles, where mostly confirmatory quantitative approaches were used. Thus, GT filled a methodological gap by providing a systematic and scientific framework for conducting exploratory inductive qualitative research, and has since become the dominant qualitative approach in many disciplines. However, GT's main purpose is and has always been, theory building from any type of data. Therefore, it is indeed an approach that may be used with qualitative data, but it would be a significant mistake to reduce it to a research methodology to be applied solely with qualitative data.

When you do research, data are essential: you need data either to confirm existing theories or to infer a new theory, as is the case for GT. However, in many methodological books, little is said about the type of data to collect and what is meant exactly by quantitative and qualitative data. The term 'quantitative data' is mostly used to describe a type of information that may be counted or expressed numerically and also used to conduct statistical analyses, whereas 'qualitative data' provide something in the form of non-numerical data. While many GT studies rely largely on qualitative data and interviews as the main method for data collection, GT can use any and all types of data, quantitative and/or qualitative, and data-collection methods, for instance observations, visual and auditory media or surveys, from any sources, e.g. reports, newspapers or answers to questionnaires.

THE DIFFERENT STREAMS OF GT

Glaser and Strauss (1967) started from a common stance about GT as a general methodology of comparative analysis for the generation of theory from empirical data in opposition to other approaches where data are collected and analyzed to verify a speculative theory. In their 1967 book, Glaser and Strauss did not provide precise guidelines for how to conduct GT but, rather, a general framework. Subsequently, and even though their collaboration had been extremely successful, each of them developed their different perspective on GT and how a GT study should be conducted, based on their original 1967 work. Various authors have since proposed different perspectives on GT, with their own guidelines and often with their own coding techniques: GT has been 'remodeled' and applied from different perspectives, and thus it is perceived and understood differently by different people. Glaser's version is known as 'Glaserian' or 'classic' GT; it is all-encompassing in its embrace of all types of data for the inductive generation of theory (Glaser, 1965; 1978; 1998; 2001; 2011; 2012; 2013; 2014a, 2014b). The other main GT approaches are those proposed by Strauss and Corbin (1998; see also Corbin and Strauss, 2014) and by Charmaz (2006, 2014a). These other approaches are mostly linked to differing underlying philosophical assumptions and are generally applied using qualitative data and methodology. While our approach in this book is in the tradition of Glaserian or classic GT, there are some fundamental principles of GT on which all authors agree:

- **Emergence**: In a GT study, the concepts must emerge from analysis of the data, not from a preconceived theoretical model based on an initial review of the extant literature.
- **Constant Comparative Analysis**: Data are analyzed and coded in search of the indicators of emerging concepts, which must be identified and systematically compared across several data slices, to merit a place in the final theory.
- **Theoretical Sampling**: All data are not collected 'up front' in a GT study, based on a predefined sample or unit, but rather they are iteratively sampled based on theoretical ideas that emerge as the data are progressively analyzed. Further data collection is guided by your need to explore and develop these ideas and the concepts they suggest as the analysis progresses.

We explore these specificities and founding principles of GT more thoroughly in Chapter 3.

If we put everything together to obtain a global picture, when you conduct a GT study, you initiate your research while remaining open to what emerges as a significant concern in the area under study, and then build an empirically-grounded theoretical explanation of how that main concern is handled. In GT, data are analyzed as they are collected using a constant comparative analysis. Additional data are theoretically sampled based on emerging conceptual ideas. The final outcome is a theory grounded in data.

In Figure 1.3 we provide a brief and simplified overview of the intermediary outcomes/results of the seven steps of the GT process towards building a grounded theory: step 1 allows the identification of the participants' main concern; step 2 allows the identification of the core category of your theory; step 3 allows the identification of the concepts related to the core category; step 4 allows you to draw the rough outline of your theoretical model; step 5 allows you to write a first draft of your theory; step 6 allows you to enrich/modify your initial model and integrate your theory in the existing literature; and step 7 allows you to produce your grounded theory. However, and contrary to what Figure 1.3 may seem to imply, the GT process is far from linear, as we will see in depth in Chapter 4.

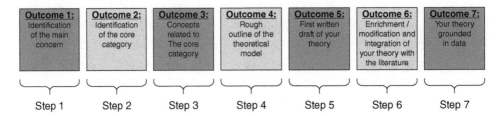

Figure 1.3 The outcomes of the seven steps of the GT process

OUTLINE OF THE REMAINDER OF THE BOOK

This book takes you step-by-step through the classic GT approach, providing all the requisite basic knowledge necessary to apply it while using any type of data, collected either in a verbal or numerical format (qualitative or quantitative data) or both.

Each chapter of the book has clear objectives highlighted through its title. At the beginning of each chapter, we propose a quote extracted from one of Barney Glaser's many books that greatly inspired us when we were new to GT. We have done this to try to pass on and share with you, some of Barney Glaser's enthusiasm about GT.

Chapter 1 has provided an overview of the GT approach. Chapter 2 discusses the place of GT, philosophically, in the management research landscape. In Chapter 3 we guide you through the basic components of a classic GT study, and then in Chapter 4 the GT research process itself. In Chapter 5 we explore three examples of classic GT in management so that you can see different applications of GT and different ways of presenting your results. Finally, in Chapter 6 we discuss the various strengths and limitations you might meet when doing classic GT.

Purposefully, we use minimal scientific jargon in the book and an accessible writing style, to allow you to concentrate on the essential purpose of your research project, i.e. to attempt producing new and useful knowledge. Important terms related to classic GT in each chapter are highlighted in bold type when they are used and explained for the first time. The majority of these terms can also be found in the glossary, provided at the end of this book.

Most of the illustrations provided in the boxes in each chapter have been inspired by our students' work while doing GT, our own GT work and/or the published GT works of colleagues. We thank our students for their insights and contributions.

We do hope this book will open the way toward many new grounded (and ground-breaking!) theories, proposed by many students.

SUMMARY

In this first chapter, we introduced GT through the different ways you can approach any research. We quickly reviewed the different streams of GT such as Strauss and Corbin's, as well as Charmaz's, and more particularly classic GT. We highlighted that while doing classic GT you may use any type of data. We also briefly introduced three fundamental principles (emergence, constant comparative analysis, and theoretical sampling) and the seven steps of the GT process. Finally, we outlined the remaining chapters.

2

UNDERSTANDING GROUNDED THEORY

'GT is tremendously empowering for those who would like to be in control in general and also in particular over the substantive area researched. The sense of empowerment is tremendous. You can explain to others what is going on.' (Glaser, 1998: 55)

INTRODUCTION

The ultimate purpose of a classic GT approach is the production of a theory, either a 'new' theory that explains some phenomenon previously unexplored or a theory that supports, enriches or contradicts other theories that were previously developed. In this chapter, we investigate the different types of theories. While we mention the philosophical debates that have been going on in the management research field for the last few decades, we highlight that classic GT is philosophically neutral and compatible with different epistemological and ontological traditions. This chapter will help you decide whether GT is appropriate for the research you have in mind.[1]

---

[1]A word of caution: Even though we (the authors of this book) do try to remain philosophically neutral when we describe classic GT, it is most probable that our own philosophical stance (critical realism) may influence and bias our writing. This book being about classic (or Glaserian) GT, it is also quite clear that we are less familiar with other ontologically-specific and remodeled versions of GT (see Chapter 1).

WHAT IS A THEORY?

In the label 'Grounded Theory', there is the word 'Theory'. So ... what is a theory?

Many different views of what a theory is have been proposed in the literature. We will retain the comprehensive definition proposed by Gregor, who views 'theories as abstract entities that aim to describe, explain, and enhance understanding of the world and, in some cases, to provide predictions of what will happen in the future and to give a basis for intervention and action' (Gregor, 2006: 616). Gregor argues that the four primary goals of a theory are analysis and description, explanation, prediction, and prescription. She shows that these goals lead to five types of theories that answer different questions: what is? (leading to an analytic theory); what is, how, why, when and where? (leading to an explanatory theory); what is and what will be? (leading to a predictive theory); what is, how, why, when, where and what will be? (leading to an explanatory and predictive theory); and how to do? (leading to a prescriptive theory for design and action). This is summarized in Table 2.1.

Table 2.1   The different types of theories

Type	Goals	Questions answered
1	Analysis and description	What is?
2	Explanation	What is, how, why, when and where?
3	Prediction	What is and what will be?
4	Explanation and prediction	What is, how, why, when, where and what will be?
5	Prescription	How to do?

Source: based on Gregor, 2006

When you develop a new theory, you can build on existing concepts/constructs ('incremental theorizing': Walsh, 2015a) or discover new concepts/constructs that you have developed through your research ('rupture theorizing': Walsh, 2015a). Incremental theorizing, although essential to help a research field mature and grow, represents additional information and gradual developments on existing concepts/constructs. Rupture theorizing uses nascent concepts/constructs, which were previously unrevealed and unstudied in the literature, or which were previously applied in, and adapted to, completely different domains. Rupture theorizing may involve defining and specifying these new concepts/constructs and/or investigating the relationships between these and other, previously established and studied, concepts/constructs. It may also use existing concepts and contradict existing literature.

Finally, when you develop a new theory – if your approach embraces realist ontological assumptions, which acknowledge the existence of other settings – you can do so at different levels of generalizability: this refers to the validity of your theory in a setting different from the one where you highlighted it. Your theory may only apply to a given context and population or it may apply to more than one context and population. When you do GT, you usually start by producing a **substantive grounded theory,** which is a theory that applies locally to the substantive area being investigated. Subsequently, a **formal grounded theory** may be generated using a substantive grounded theory as the basis for more formal theory development that is applicable to many different substantive areas and diversified populations. This would, of course, imply collecting further slices of data from different substantive areas. Thus, a formal grounded theory is a theory that can be applied in different contexts. Deciding on pursuing a formal GT is often the result of finding the **core category** of a previous substantive theory, i.e. the category that appears to explain significantly how the main concern is processed, managed or resolved, and theoretically sampling for it in other substantive areas. Indeed, once the core category has been found, the researcher often starts to see their core category in many different contexts, hence a call for more research toward a formal grounded theory. This call for generalization is one of the most important triggers to generate a formal grounded theory.

For a master's student, generating a well-developed substantive theory, with one core category and four or five related concepts, is usually sufficient. If any, the potential formal theory is usually mentioned in the future research section of the master's thesis.

In Box 2.1, we provide several illustrations of the potential passage from a substantive to a formal grounded theory.

Box 2.1   Illustrations of the potential passage from substantive to formal grounded theory

Glaser and Strauss first developed a substantive theory related to the substantive area of dying patients (*Awareness of dying*, 1965). They then extended their core category (change of patients' status from living to dying) to build a formal theory of status passage (Glaser & Strauss, 1971) that was related and applicable to many different substantive areas as diverse as education, career, chronic disease or marriage.

Holton (2007) presents a grounded theory of rehumanizing knowledge work; however, further developing this substantive theory as a formal theory is quite feasible given the many social arenas where rehumanizing exists, arenas as diverse as the slow food movement, therapeutic communities, rehabilitation services, and compassionate care settings.

Mourmant and Voutsina (2017) work on a substantive grounded theory related to (future) entrepreneurs, and how the concept of entrepreneurial mind-shift helps understand how an employee makes the decision to quit their job and become an entrepreneur. However, a mind-shift can be highlighted not only in the context of entrepreneurship, like in Mourmant and Voutsina (2017), but also in the broader context of changing careers or in the even broader context of any decision-making process. Ultimately, this could then lead to some formal grounded theories of greater scope than the original substantive grounded theory.

Walsh (2014) studies causal relationships between IT use and users' IT culture and IT needs. Some of these relationships are only confirmed and valid in the investigated context and population with some specific IT: they are relevant to the substantive grounded theory proposed in this article. Other relationships appear to be consistent regardless of the context, population and IT investigated: they could then be part of a more formal grounded theory.

WHAT ARE GT'S PHILOSOPHICAL ASSUMPTIONS?

Over the last few decades, there has been an important debate about the rationale for combining quantitative and qualitative data, data-collection methods, and analysis techniques, which some consider as incompatible due to philosophical assumptions and the different worldviews presumed to be linked to them. Quantitative purists tend to espouse a positivist philosophy with independent and dependent variables, and quantitative data. These quantitative purists consider that the observer is separate from their object of study; for them, science is considered objective and aims to uncover laws that are time and context-free; their focus is on deduction, confirmation, hypothesis testing, and quantitative analysis. Causality between two variables is understood from a fairly simplistic perspective ('A causes B'), often without taking into account the possible influence of the context or of the people within that context. Qualitative purists often espouse a philosophical position usually combining interpretivism and constructivism with some forms of case research, interpreting settings and contexts to take the research participants' perspectives. These purists consider that there is not one single reality but that realities are multiple and socially constructed, so that knower and known cannot be separated; for them, research is subjective and value-bound; causes and effects cannot be differentiated and their focus is on induction, exploration, discovery, and qualitative analysis (Johnson & Onwuegbuzie, 2004).

However, neither of the two extreme positions described above is a comprehensive expression of the management research world of today or a true vision of what positivism and interpretivism/constructivism mean. They also ignore other philosophical perspectives that have emerged - for instance, post-positivism, pragmatism or critical realism - that accept and/or mix qualitative and quantitative data, data-collection methods and analysis techniques.

Furthermore, and whatever their philosophical perspectives and/or the purpose of their research, many researchers have reached some agreement on certain major issues regarding theorizing. Whether they use qualitative and/or quantitative data and analysis techniques and even if their philosophical assumptions may vary:

- reasoning is relative and varies among people;
- observation is an approximation of reality;
- a single set of empirical data can yield different befitting theories;
- hypotheses are linked to assumptions;
- probabilistic evidence is not final proof; and
- researchers' beliefs are embedded in the assumptions of their respective communities.

One of the reasons that may explain why extreme purist positions have developed, is that philosophical assumptions have been mapped mainly as an opposition between induction and deduction, as well as between general or universal perspectives (nomothetic) – looking for universal laws that are statistically verified – and more local perspectives (idiographic) looking for theories that are locally true in a given context with selected people. The simplistic coupling of quantitative data and analysis techniques with a universal deductive approach, versus qualitative data and analysis techniques with a more local inductive approach, creates an unnecessary and artificial opposition between unrealistic extreme positions. Box 2.2 provides an illustration of why we believe these extreme positions are not adequate representations of any philosophical perspective.

Box 2.2   Newton's story, or why caricatures are not a good representation of philosophical perspectives

The story goes that while Isaac Newton (a famous English mathematician, physicist and key figure in the scientific revolution) sat under a tree, an apple fell at his feet (this incident in itself may be considered as data resulting from participant observation). Newton himself stated on a number of occasions that watching the apple fall from the tree inspired and led him to induce and formulate his theory of gravitation, which subsequently became a universal law.

Even though simplified to the extreme for our purpose, this example is a good one to show how exploration (openness to new data, such as the fall of an apple at one's feet) and induction (looking for the rule that governs the fall) may lead to the development of a universal law, and thus why the extreme positions that have fed heated debates in the management field are not relevant philosophical perspectives.

Confirmatory theory-driven research and exploratory data-driven research have to be differentiated, and GT is clearly exploratory and data-driven. However, doing GT does not imply either a local (idiographic) or general/universal (nomothetic) perspective; while remaining in an exploratory stance, both are possible. If we map research along the two axes Exploration–Confirmation and General–Local, it is then clear that any Grounded Theory research should be positioned in one of the two lower quadrants in Figure 2.1. Furthermore, and as highlighted in this figure, idiographic, substantive grounded theories can lead to different types of nomothetic, formalized grounded theories, using any kind of data (qualitative and/or quantitative) while maintaining an exploratory, data-driven stance.

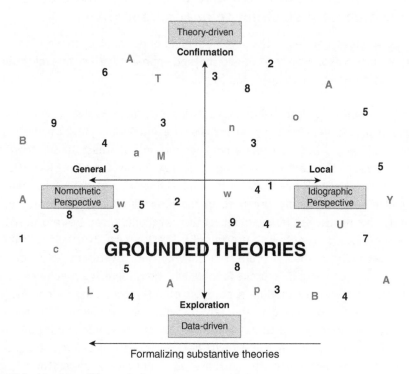

Figure 2.1   Mapping GT research

Source: adapted from Walsh et al., 2015b

Thus, we can view GT as a general methodology for research (Holton, 2008), and in the same way that GT is flexible in relation to the types of data, data-collection methods and analysis techniques that can be used, GT is also philosophically flexible, accommodating any philosophical perspective as espoused by the researcher (Holton & Walsh, 2017). The researcher's philosophical stance comes into play in what they may choose as their initial area of interest and what they consider to be appropriate data sources, but GT can be applied to any data whether those data are viewed as inter-preted or objective. What is important for the grounded theorist is the discovery of concepts that lie within the data.

As the three authors of this book happen to be critical realists – which means we view the world as accommodating human agents, who are able to shape the reality that confronts others – we provide an example of classic GT applied with a critical realist philosophical stance in Box 2.3 below. Indeed, and as explained in Chapter 1, many other philosophical stances and approaches are possible.

Box 2.3   Illustration of the use of GT with mixed data and a critical realist philosophical perspective

Walsh (2014) clearly states at the very beginning of her article, 'In a critical realist stance, we use an exploratory GT mixed-method approach with both qualitative and quantitative data.' She then proceeds to explain:

> ... it is ... essential to clarify what causality is for a critical realist. The notion of causality as a 'generative mechanism' is a core and defining feature of critical realism (Bhaskar, 2002). Generative mechanisms are best understood as 'tendencies', as their activation is highly context-dependent (Bhaskar, 2002). In contrast with the Humean (from the philosopher Hume) vision of causality ('A causes B'), commonly accepted in the Information Systems traditional quantitative positivist circles, a generative mechanism can be reformulated as 'A generates B in context C' (Cartwright, 2003; Smith, 2010). For a critical realist causality is, thus, a process of how causal powers are actualized in some particular context: a process in which the generative mechanisms of that context (C) shape (modulate, dampen, etc.) the particular outcomes. For instance ... a car will drive adequately if it has four wheels and an engine, but only if somebody also turns on the ignition and a nail does not puncture one of its tires. Therefore, the arrows (between constructs) in the diagrams proposed ... do not illustrate causality as traditionally understood; they illustrate the activation of causal powers as revealed in the substantive area (the use of the Moodle platform by students and professors) and the context (a European business school) that were investigated. The paths that are reported in the models ... are those that best fitted our set of data (qualitative and quantitative) within the substantive area and the context that were being investigated [Substantive theory].

> Where possible, however, we ... extended our results in order for them to be applied in further research in other substantive areas and contexts.

When we understood the collected data as sufficient to demonstrate that a proposition would apply whatever the substantive area and context investigated, we added the word 'mostly' in the wording of the corresponding proposition. 'Mostly' is, however, used only as a heuristic device, and should not be taken at face value. It means that, based on the data we collected, the proposition appears to extend to other substantive areas and other contexts beyond those researched for the present study [Formal theory]; this would, of course, need to be verified in further research. When 'mostly' is not used in the wording of a proposition, it indicates that the corresponding proposition may hold true only within our substantive area and investigated context.

SHOULD YOU USE GT?

As long as it is grounded (i.e. rooted) in data, a grounded theory, the end result of the classic GT research process, can be any of the types of theories described at the beginning of this chapter, except for type 1 (analysis and description). Type 1 theories are excluded because, even though it might start with description, a classic grounded theory should go beyond description towards conceptualization.

The sources of a grounded theory are found in empirical data, not in pre-existing theories. Data for a grounded theory are understood as any element related to the phenomenon of interest, which the researcher can collect and code/conceptualize. Data can be collected through any data-collection method (e.g. interviews, surveys, web search engines, fieldnotes, etc.) in numerical or verbal format. For instance, data could be interview transcripts, music, pictures, films, answers to a survey, quotes from famous authors, etc.

Doing GT, the researcher turns directly to empirical data in an exploratory inductive stance, whereas in a hypothetical-deductive stance, the literature is usually first investigated for clues to lay down a hypotheses in a linear research approach, often leading to incremental theorizing. As all preconceptions are to be set aside when doing GT (Glaser, 2013), adopting a GT stance often leads to theorizing in rupture with existing literature.

The intent in GT is to approach a subject inductively with as few preconceived ideas about the phenomenon as possible. As such, if a concept/construct has never been previously studied in a field, the literature will be of little help to describe or explain it or to develop propositions/hypotheses involving this new construct. Alternatively, if existing concepts are used, investigating the literature *ex ante* could lead to conceptual pollution and work as a barrier to emergence and the researcher's creativity.

Hence, you probably should *not* use GT in the following cases:

- If the phenomenon you are investigating is already well covered in the literature and if you plan to use only existing concepts/variables already proposed in the literature (incremental theorizing) without allowing for new concepts and/or new relationships to emerge from your data.
- If you deduct hypotheses from existing theories and you solely plan to verify these hypotheses (confirmatory research).

An illustration of a research that is probably unsuited to a GT approach is provided in Box 2.4.

Box 2.4   Illustration of a research unsuited to a GT approach

Jonathan wishes to study how the perceptions of employees about the way they are supervised influences their knowledge-hiding behaviors. Knowledge hiding has been investigated in the literature and proposed to be assessed through three dimensions (evasive hiding, playing dumb and rationalized hiding: Connelly et al., 2012). Perception of supervision has also been investigated in the literature, e.g. abusive supervision (Peng et al., 2014). Questionnaires to assess these constructs are also readily available in the literature. Then, Jonathan can lay down the hypothesis that abusive supervision will have a significant positive influence on employees' knowledge-hiding behaviors (the more a supervisor is perceived as abusive, the more employees will be inclined to hide the knowledge they possess) and collect quantitative data through a survey. He can then investigate correlations between the two variables (knowledge hiding and abusive supervision) or effect a linear regression of one variable on the other to verify if his hypothesis is confirmed or not.

Jonathan uses deductions from existing theories to lay down some hypotheses that he intends to verify. This is clearly a confirmatory hypothetico-deductive approach and not suited to a GT study, which should start with no preconceptions and remain exploratory throughout all of the research process.

You could consider using GT in the following cases:

- If the literature of the domain that interests you does not allow drawing hypotheses related to the phenomenon you are investigating, e.g. if the phenomenon is very complex, completely new, or if it is not new but has never been investigated. This last situation is relatively rare in management science at master's level.

- If the phenomenon you are investigating is already well covered in the literature, but you would like a new perspective on this phenomenon that might lead you to contradict or complement existing research (rupture theorizing).

- If you would like to investigate data in an exploratory fashion, without assuming that previous research should automatically apply and without laying down any hypotheses beforehand (exploratory research).

Illustrations of some research that may be compatible with a classic GT approach are provided in Box 2.5.

Box 2.5 Illustrations of research suited to a GT approach

Carole wishes to investigate digital culture at the level of individuals. She has searched the literature and found some previous works that investigated this phenomenon at group level, but nothing at the level of the individual. She then decides to take an exploratory inductive approach and intends to start collecting data through interviews.

Nicholas wishes to investigate well-being at work, and if it could be nurtured. Well-being is a phenomenon already investigated in the positive psychology literature. However, Nicolas wishes to take a different perspective, not to assume that some variables are significant in relation to well-being at work, and adopt an exploratory inductive approach. He intends to use quantitative secondary data extracted from answers to surveys conducted in the firm where he interned, and then apply exploratory data-mining techniques on these data.

Finally, using GT as a research approach requires that you have some skills (Glaser, 1992):

- You have to be able to step back from the data and conceptualize them, which Glaser (1978) termed **theoretical sensitivity**, or the capacity to conceptualize and formulate a theory as it emerges from data; this is an essential skill that results from the interplay of your creativity and acquired analysis techniques, the creative element being significant.

- You must be able to tolerate some amount of confusion, be comfortable with complexity, and remain open to what you find in your data.
- You must be able to avoid being tempted to force preconceived ideas or frameworks gleaned from published literature upon your data, as these could block or pollute an emerging theory.

These skills are essential if you wish to use GT as your research approach.

SUMMARY

In this second chapter, we defined what is meant by the word 'theory' and the five types of theories that serve different purposes: analysis and description, explanation, prediction, explanation and prediction, and prescription. We clarified that classic GT can be adopted with any philosophical stance. We highlighted that classic GT is clearly exploratory and data-driven. We introduced the notion of core category, and discussed the differences between substantive grounded theory and formal grounded theory, and when you should consider using GT. Finally, we presented some of the skills needed to conduct a GT study.

3

BASIC COMPONENTS OF A CLASSIC GROUNDED THEORY APPROACH

'Doing GT rejuvenated her life and her mind. She was having fun.'
(Glaser, 1998: 62)

INTRODUCTION

What are the main differentiating specificities and components of classic GT? How do you code data when doing classic GT? This chapter answers these questions. It is divided into three main sections: in the first section we discuss three differentiating and fundamental principles of a GT approach; in the second we highlight memoing as an essential element when conducting a GT study; and in the third we describe the different types of coding used in classic GT to help understand the collected data.

THE MAIN SPECIFICITIES OF GT

While the end purpose of a GT study is indeed theory building, there are three fundamental principles that may be considered as differentiating the GT approach from other research approaches:

- Emergence - concepts and relationships come from the data and are not preconceived or imposed on data.

- Constant comparative analysis – data are continuously compared with previously collected and analyzed data, looking for similarities and differences to facilitate conceptualization and theorization.
- Theoretical sampling – sampling is directed by the emerging theory and continues until no new relevant information is revealed by new data.

These fundamental principles of GT require you to become intimate with your data and their conceptual underpinnings for substantive theory development. You have to make sure these three principles are respected while conducting GT research, regardless of which type of data are being used.

Emergence

GT is a general methodology (Holton, 2008) that aims to help the discovery of new theories. The researcher enters the field and explores a substantive area. In everyday terms, a substantive area is a domain or a phenomenon that has substance and involves matters of major or practical importance to all concerned (*Merriam-Webster's* dictionary). In GT terms, a substantive area usually involves a specific context and a specific population, which are being studied. The issues or problems of those actively engaged as participants in the research project are investigated to allow the emergence of their main concern. This main issue becomes the basis for the articulation of a grounded theory that explains how the issue is processed or resolved by the participants. GT does not require as a starting point to identify a gap in the literature from which precise research questions are framed to guide the study. It requires being flexible and open to discovery.

While doing GT, concepts and variables come from the data; they are not preconceived or imposed on data. There should be no 'forcing', where it is assumed that particular constructs/variables will occur in the data and are significant for the emerging theory. Thus, and whatever the data that are being used, exploration and emergence of the theory from the data have to remain central. Variables should emerge from the data as relevant to the substantive area that is being investigated and not be assumed and forced into the analysis. Emergence necessitates that you remain open to discovering the main concern motivating the interest or action within the area you study. The actual research question of your thesis (that answers a gap in the literature) is not predefined; it will probably only emerge at the end of the GT research process, once the first draft of your theory has been written and you compare it to existing literature.

Constant comparative analysis

The constant comparative analysis of empirical data, as you collect them, with previously collected data is fundamental to doing GT. Constant comparison requires concepts to earn their way into a grounded theory through the **interchangeability of indicators**. The interchangeability of indicators refers to the construction of saturated 'multi-indicators concepts' (Glaser, 1978: 65) opposed to 'one-indicator concepts' which are merely an illustration or a conjecture of a non-grounded concept. The roots of the interchangeability of indicators may be found in latent structure/ class analysis and the index formation process, used mostly with quantitative data, as developed at Columbia University's School of Applied Arts under the leadership of Paul Lazarsfeld (Lazarsfeld & Henry, 1968). It also finds its roots in *explication de texte*, used with qualitative data, as taught in the Sorbonne University in France, where Glaser spent some time studying. *Explication de texte* refers to 'reading closely line by line to ascertain what exactly the author is saying' (Glaser, 1998: 24).

In Box 3.1 we provide some illustrations of the interchangeable indicators of some concepts.

Box 3.1 Illustrations of the interchangeability of indicators toward conceptualization

Walsh (2014) found that the two items below, extracted from interviews, were interchangeable indicators of the multi-indicator concept she named 'Global IT needs':

'Information technology is part of my day-to-day life, and I would rather not do without it'

'I need IT in all aspects of my life, and I don't wish to do without it'

When applied with quantitative data, these indicators were used as items of the corresponding reflective construct.

Anouk wrote her master's thesis on the fast casual restaurant – a type of restaurant between the fast food and the casual restaurant. She found that 'Transparency' is an important concept for the client. This concept of transparency emerged several times, both through her observations and from interviews with clients and entrepreneurs. Below are the interchangeable indicators for 'Transparency', which Anouk identified from different sources (observations and interviews). She conceptualized and coded all these items as 'Transparency':

The preparation of the meal is done in front of the clients. (Anouk's observation)

The kitchens are half or completely opened. (Anouk's observation)

(Continued)

(Continued)

'The client wants to check that the criteria of hygiene are respected in the kitchens, such as wearing hat and gloves.' (interview with a client)

'The only thing between the client and the kitchen is a transparent window.' (interview with a client)

'Having an open kitchen is very reassuring for the client.' (interview with an entrepreneur)

An **incident** is 'something dependent on or subordinate to' the phenomenon you are investigating, an 'occurrence' (*Merriam-Webster's* dictionary) of something that emerges from your data and strikes the researcher as being remarkable and noteworthy. For example, drawing upon Box 3.1, an incident could be a client remembering the open kitchen as something reassuring about their last meal at a fast casual restaurant. The researcher will then compare this incident with an incident highlighted by another client. In our example, it could be, the hats and gloves that this other client could have seen kitchen staff wearing, during a different meal at a different fast casual restaurant. You may then stumble on indicators such as 'The only thing between the client and the kitchen is a transparent window' and 'I like to be able to check that the criteria of hygiene are respected in the kitchens.' By comparing these two indicators, you then realize that they are interchangeable, as they both point to the emerging concept of transparency. You also notice that other indicators may be highlighted in the same incident or sentence (e.g. hygiene in our example). After comparing many incidents, there will be saturation of the concept of transparency. Then, by using the same technique, you can move on to the dimensions and properties of this new concept as well as how the concepts are interrelated, e.g. hygiene may be indicated through other incidents and be one of the reasons for this desire for transparency.

Below is a short description of one loop of constant comparative analysis for the emergence of one concept (including its properties and dimensions) based on the comparison of incidents. Please note that this technique is used iteratively throughout the entire GT research process to help and allow for the emergence of the various concepts, core category, and relationships.

Empirical incidents are compared, incident to incident, to identify indicators of new concepts.

When many indicators become interchangeable, they lead to a pattern.

This pattern is simply named – it becomes an emerging concept.

Additional empirical incidents are compared to the emerging concepts, to build and substantiate these with their properties and dimensions.

When further data yield no additional elaboration of properties and dimensions of emerging concepts, saturation of these concepts is considered as having been achieved. Constant comparison continues, and the concepts are then related to each other to generate potential relationships, further expressed as propositions/hypotheses. Thus, the constant comparative analysis of data threads throughout the entire GT process, from the initial data collected through to the full integration of the generated theory that is integrated and consistent with all collected data.

For those of you who work with quantitative data, it may be useful to highlight that fully interchangeable indicators are items that allow the assessment of a reflective (sometimes named 'Type A') construct. However, some indicators are not *stricto sensu* interchangeable, while at the same time pointing at the same concept, for instance the dimensions of a concept, which point at a formative construct (sometimes named 'Type B') if you use quantitative terminology. When dealing with the dimensions of a concept, each indicator is necessary to fully define the concept, but they illustrate different components of this concept. This differentiation between the two different types of constructs is particularly important if you start with qualitative data but eventually intend to use quantitative data and some statistical analysis techniques, e.g. partial least squares path modeling. Ideally, when dealing with indicators pointing at the dimensions of a formative construct, each dimension should be individually conceptualized through further interchangeable indicators to guarantee saturation.

In Box 3.2 we provide an illustration of the coding and conceptualization of the dimensions of a concept.

Box 3.2   Illustration of indicators of the dimensions of a concept

We continue with Anouk's thesis already mentioned in Box 3.1 about the fast casual restaurants. After Anouk coded her interviews, observations and fieldnotes, she came up with the following specific criteria or dimensions for the concept 'Quality of products' for a fast casual restaurant:

(Dimension 1) Fresh products

(Dimension 2) Healthy products

(Dimension 3) Dietetic products

(Continued)

(Continued)

(Dimension 4) Organic products

(Dimension 5) Respect for the various types of diet

(Dimension 6) Nutritious products

Theoretical sampling

Constant comparative analysis, described above, and theoretical sampling described in this subsection, are intimately linked and represent an iterative process. Many research approaches require that you sample up front before you start your research, a population that is statistically representative of the whole population you wish to study. This is not the case when you do GT: you first start with an area, a domain or topic that interests you with no preconceived problem or issue in your mind (Glaser, 1992). As you collect and code your first set of data – without any preconception – you will start to see the emergence of the participants' main concern and, potentially, a core category. After the core category has emerged (step 3 of Figure 1.3), you can start to use theoretical sampling, which means that as you constantly compare your data, you will sample further data guided by the emerging theory (theoretical sampling). In other words, when analyzing the data you have already collected, you will decide what data to collect next and where to find these in order to develop your theory as it is emerging.

Hence, theoretical sampling is not guided by statistical significance or by a preconceived theoretical framework. It is guided by conceptual emergence and relevance while limited by the saturation of the concepts and their properties/dimensions. Consequently, selection of data sources is neither a random selection nor totally predetermined. Additional data are selected in the service of the emerging theory as you gather additional data related to emerging patterns, by asking specific questions. You might also choose to return to data already collected, review these, recode and selectively sample them for the emerging pattern. In other words, you will deduce from your previous results where to sample next. Theoretical sampling is a deductive process in an otherwise overall inductive research approach.

When you collect data by theoretical sampling, the questions (asked during interviews or as part of a survey) guide the collection of data to fill in gaps and extend the theory that has started to emerge from previously collected data. Therefore, your theory is more likely to emerge and be integrated fully. Theoretical sampling will reduce the amount of data you will need because further data collection is focused. However, if you sample inadequately, it will be obvious at once, as your new data will not enrich the emerging theory.

The questions to ask yourself when you theoretically sample are: *What groups or sub-groups should I investigate next? For what purpose, linked to what I have already found?* Intergroup similarities and differences are important as they may point at the conditions under which categories and their properties vary and to what degree they vary.

Through theoretical sampling, you will use several slices of data, which you can collect using different data sources, locations, participants or interviewing styles, and which are determined only by the necessity of theoretical relevance and coverage. When theoretically sampling quantitative data, and when software is used for some of the analyses, you should reflectively ensure that the mathematical algorithms in the software do not eliminate some 'statistically insignificant' cases or groups of cases without investigating them, with the help of qualitative data previously collected or specifically collected for this purpose. In Box 3.3, we provide an illustration of theoretical sampling and its importance to help theorizing.

Box 3.3   An example of theoretical sampling

In Chapter 1, Mary's research was briefly described in Box 1.1 and 1.2. Through abductive logic, Mary had found that age was a significant variable to take into account to explain IT acculturation because, overall, the young people she had interviewed at first tended to be more IT acculturated and at ease with new technologies than older people in her sample. Purposely, she then proceeded to sample further and interview young people, who appeared to be little, or not at all, IT acculturated, and elderly people, who behaved like IT 'geeks' and were very attracted to IT. This allowed her to highlight other variables that appeared more significant than age to explain a high level of IT acculturation for these people.

MEMOING

Writing is part of the GT research process, starting from the beginning of the research and continuing until the end. Through all of the GT process you will write **memos** to help the analysis of your data and conceptualization. Memos, the notes you write about the data, the concepts/categories and the connections/relationships between them, are written throughout the constant comparative process to capture your emerging ideas. Memoing is done in tandem with coding. In your memos, you will explain how the data indicate a concept or property of a concept and how this concept relates to other concepts. Thus, when doing GT, writing and thinking are embedded and intertwined. The writing of memos helps you to tell the story found in your data as it unfolds; it helps you to stay focused and not risk losing sight of important elements that you have witnessed and/or perceived.

Through memo writing, you explore the data creatively to reveal subtle patterns of social behavior. Memo writing is a continual process that helps to raise the data to a conceptual level and develop the properties of each category. Memoing your ideas as you code is essential to keep your analysis on a conceptual level and not to simply produce a descriptive account. Memos are works in progress, intended to capture ideas as they emerge without the worries of writing style, grammar and spelling that can cause some writers to freeze their thinking. As Glaser (1978) suggests, the goals in memoing are to stimulate and capture conceptual ideas that emerge from coding and constant comparative analysis, and to build up a rich fund of captured ideas that facilitate later theoretical integration during the theoretical coding stage.

Memoing as you code your data will help you to discover what is actually happening in the situation you are investigating. For instance, in a memo related to a given interview, you can indicate if you feel that the interviewee is offering an account of their own experience, a reflection on that experience, a projection of someone else's experience, or a 'revised' corporate version. All of these are possible and interesting in themselves, but it is important to know what type of data you are collecting and why you are collecting this type of data, and what these data are really telling you about the phenomenon you are studying.

In the same way as you group and sort your data when you code them, memos need to be sorted regularly in order to avoid information overload and being 'drowned' in data. This sorting into 'piles of data' or 'piles of memos' can be done physically on a table or on your computer with the help of a word processor or some other software (see Figure 3.1).

Figure 3.1   Sorting piles of empirical data and memos physically on a table
Source: Walsh, 2014

Some researchers will also mix these two methods to get the best of both worlds. Some find that the physical act of hand sorting memos facilitates the processing of matured ideas, helps the integration of these ideas into a global picture and, thus, guides the organization and integration of the overall theory.

In Box 3.4 we provide an illustration of a memo extracted from a master's student's dissertation.

Box 3.4   Illustration of a memo (Source: Tiers et al., 2013)

Grégoire Tiers studied cloud computing for his master's thesis. Below is a memo he wrote about the core category that emerged from his data. This memo was written after the sorting process and was integrated into the final publication of an article in a top journal of the Information Systems research field:

'Maturation appears to be the core category of this sorting. This phenomenon of maturation towards cloud computing emerged at four levels, as evidenced by the identification of four types of maturity: maturity of the organization, security maturity, maturity of the technical solution, and maturity of the legal environment.

The analysis of the data also shows that the different maturities are organized around configurations, where each configuration is composed of different types of maturity at different degrees.'

Sorting may also lead you to more memo writing as you begin to see and record the relationships among concepts. This helps to raise further the conceptual level of the theory and reduces the potential for you to slip into description.

To provide a simple summary of the specificities that should be found in any GT study, we illustrate these below, using the GT tree metaphor (see Figure 3.2).

CODING DATA WHILE DOING CLASSIC GT

In order to be able to apply grounded theory in the analysis, it is important to give some thought to the way in which the data are collected. Thus, in this section, we first investigate data collection, and the coding to be applied to these data to facilitate conceptualization while doing GT.

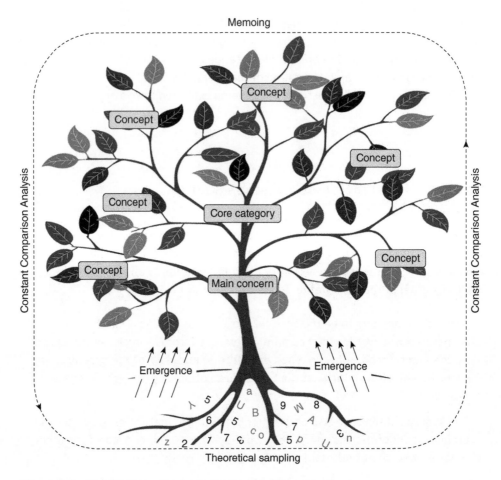

Figure 3.2   The GT Tree – the basic tenets of a GT approach

Data collection

GT studies that rely on qualitative data often feature interviews as a primary source of data, but you can also use informal conversations with participants, or data collected during meetings that you attended as a participant observer. By capturing or remembering a few keywords during a conversation or a meeting, you can later write up a fieldnote elaborating your ideas, which you can then code and memo. If you start with quantitative data, there will probably be secondary data, already collected for other purposes, e.g. databases collected by public bodies and made available to researchers, together with the questionnaires used to collect those data. If you start with qualitative data and then decide to move on to quantitative data with a questionnaire based on the qualitative data you previously collected, you will then be able to collect primary quantitative data, specifically for your purpose.

For instance, you could build a survey using participants' accounts and administer it to a wide spectrum of people.

In collecting interview or informal conversation data for a GT study, all that is needed is one 'grand tour' question (Simmons, 2010) – something as simple and open as 'Tell me about your job/family/hobby?' or 'What's it like to work here?' etc. A 'grand tour' question gives the participant an opportunity to tell you about what it is they would like to talk about. As the researcher, your challenge is to follow where they want to take the conversation and to probe with more specific follow up questions such as, 'Tell me more about the time when...', 'How do you handle ... ?', and 'Tell me about what went well when...'. You will have to find the trigger that starts the person talking openly about what concerns or interests them. Your goal here is to *tone the conversation* so that the participant feels comfortable in opening up and sharing with you. It is important for you not to dominate the conversation. The less you talk, the more likely you are to identify the participants' main concern. If there is a pause in the conversation, wait a moment or two and then softly encourage the individual to continue. You might also repeat the last few words they have said and then wait. Be patient. Ensure that the interviewee has time to feel comfortable in opening up to you.

Classic GT does not require you to audio record and transcribe interviews. Note taking to capture key phrases and ideas that the participant raises is sufficient. However, you might find that audio recording and transcribing interviews in writing are required by your supervisor or your institution as proof of the research that you have conducted, and as reassurance that your data are indeed grounded in reality and not invented. It is also a good means by which to assess your competence in interviewing. Finally, and in any case, you might find it easier and more productive, especially at the beginning of your research, to audio record and transcribe your interviews whenever possible in order to be able to immerse yourself into them again and reflect on their content in some detail, after you have conducted the interviews. Something that might not have appeared sufficiently important at first to you to be noted, might subsequently reveal itself to be essential and, if you do not audio record audio and transcribe, you might lose or oversee some interesting data that could lengthen your work unnecessarily. You can also audio record interviews and only transcribe verbatim and ideas that you consider relevant and interesting.

As your study progresses, and if your supervisor allows it, you might move on to simply keeping fieldnotes of relevant concepts and ideas: if something is relevant to your theory, it will be mentioned, or you will notice it in several interviews – these are multiple indicators of a concept – as your research progresses. Whatever your supervisor and institution require, you have to be aware that audio recording a full interview sets up a different dynamic where the participant may respond differently to questions when they know their answers are being recorded. Some might become nervous about being recorded and some may 'edit' their responses so as not to deviate from what they feel is expected of them as a participant. This is why, in GT, it is also often helpful to re-interview some participants as your study progresses. Re-interviewing is a form of theoretical sampling that can add important depth to your emerging theory. Re-interviewing can be also especially helpful where your access to data is limited to a very specific population or a sensitive area of research interest (e.g. transgender youth, harassment, etc.). Also, once your core category has emerged, you may wish to return to those participants that you interviewed earlier in your research to probe more specifically around the emergent core. You might say something like 'In some of my conversations with others, they have mentioned ... has this been your experience? Can you tell me more about what happened?', etc. As such, re-interviewing can be a valuable way of theoretically sampling to elaborate the properties and dimensions of your emergent core concept.

It is worth highlighting that capturing interview data in full detail through audio recording and transcribing is not mandatory when doing classic GT and can actually sometimes detract from producing a quality grounded theory. The potential derailing occurs on two levels. Firstly, audio recording can inhibit participants who may resort to 'properlining' data, i.e. they would only reveal what they think is proper and correct (Glaser, 1998: 110). Secondly, the time and tedium involved in transcribing *in extenso* may divert your energy and attention to full descriptive capture of the data rather than its abstract conceptualization for theory development. In this process, your creativity in analyzing and conceptualizing the data may well be inhibited (Glaser, 1998: 112).

When you use primary quantitative data, you will investigate your emerging theory and model as you collect your data. For instance, as a questionnaire is administered and the answers to the questionnaire start coming in, you can check on the possible saturation of a concept through repeated exploratory factor analyses as well as the assessment of Cronbach's alphas to guide the elimination of some items from your questionnaire. This in turn will sometimes guide you toward the need for further data collection.

Data coding

There are two types of coding in classic GT - **substantive coding** (which includes **open coding** and **selective coding**) and **theoretical coding**. When you do substantive coding, you code for concepts. When you do theoretical coding, you code for relationships between concepts. Substantive coding, which begins with the first data collected, aims to conceptualize the empirical substance of your data, i.e. to highlight the concepts that emerge from the data. Theoretical coding integrates emergent concepts in a model that explains the pattern of relationships between the concepts. This second type of coding is usually reserved for the latter stage of the GT process.

The different types of coding to be effected while doing classic GT are summarized in Table 3.1 and described and illustrated below.

Table 3.1 The coding effected in a classic GT approach

Types of coding			Description	Purpose	Results
Substantive (Coding for concepts)		Open	In vivo codes: Derived directly from the words of your participants and capturing what is going on Analytic codes: Conceptualizing what is happening	To identify in the data 'incidents' that appear to indicate one or more concepts	Main concern & core category
		Selective	Coding around the core category	To identify the concepts related to the core category, its dimensions and properties	Saturation of core category and its related concepts
Theoretical (Coding for relationships between concepts)			Coding to model the relationships between and among the core category and related concepts	To shape the theory	Conceptual model of the grounded theory

Open coding

We begin the substantive coding process with open coding of empirical data. To 'open code', we identify in the data, 'incidents' that appear to indicate one or more concepts and we label these, using one or two words per code – including verbs and gerunds (words formed with verbs but acting as nouns, e.g. 'hurrying', 'remaining', etc.) – to capture the action. We can aim to capture exactly what is going on in a highlighted incident using the language of the domain or the exact words of the participants (e.g. remaining composed) as a first stage to identify a concept, and/ or aim to explain conceptually what is happening (e.g. identity maintenance) as the next stage of conceptual abstraction.

Even though it is sometimes challenging to move from descriptive codes to more conceptual ones, the close reading of collected data and constant comparison of incidents in the data for the interchangeability of conceptual indicators should allow concepts to be identified, and their conceptual level elevated and eventually saturated. One must ensure that no important concepts are bypassed and that concepts do emerge from the collected data rather than be assumed, based on existing literature.

When you open code, you should constantly compare emerging incidents, noting similarities and differences and looking for patterns emerging in the coded data. The more you code, the more you should begin to see some patterns emerging from your data and the same conceptual interchangeable indicators (codes) recurring across most of your collected data. Coding is an intuitive comparison of indicators. Once you begin to see the same patterns over and over, you stop coding. There is no finite resolution here as there is always the possibility that new elements could emerge with more data analysis, but as the theorist you use your intuition to decide when you have done enough. Of course, there will always also be the constraints of the time you have available and the expectations of your supervisors in terms of the rigour of your emergent theory.

For open coding to be productive, you have to suspend any preconceived notions about what the data should reveal. When you approach the data, you will not 'know' what you are going to find. To avoid remaining at a purely descriptive stage and to help you conceptualize, keep asking yourself the following neutral questions: 'What is this data a study of?', 'What concept or category does this incident indicate?', 'What is actually happening in the data?', 'What is the issue facing the participants?', 'What is their main concern and how do they manage or resolve it?'

A **concept** is an abstract or generic idea generalized from particular instances (*Webster* dictionary). In the context of GT, a category is a 'type of concept, usually used for a higher level of abstraction' (Glaser, 1992: 38). Based on the concepts that emerge from the data, you must raise the level of conceptualization and turn your concepts into categories. However, it must be highlighted that Glaser (2011) often uses the words code, concept, property and **category** as synonymous. In Boxes 3.5 and 3.6 we provide illustrations of conceptualized verbatim that are further categorized.

Box 3.5 Open coding from verbatim to conceptualization, then to category

If you look at the interview illustrated in Figure 3.4 at the end of this chapter, the verbatim 'I felt I was insufficiently qualified' was conceptualized as 'insufficiency of qualification' and further categorized as a 'driver' to studying for a DBA.

To help you see emerging patterns in your coding, you have to keep moving through the data rather than ponder too long on any one incident. Refinement of concepts and categories is ongoing. Therefore, you should not fret during the actual GT research process about the specific labels that you use as you open code. You can use any labels that will help you capture the idea. There will be time later in the process, and when your full theory has emerged, to fine-tune the labels for concepts and categories.

Box 3.6 Illustration of concept emergence and conceptualizations during open coding (Source: Lohse, 2018; defended DBA dissertation)

Hendrik is studying why managers currently working quite successfully in firms may choose to invest time in doctoral studies and enroll in doctoral programs. Here are some examples of his conceptualization through collected interview verbatims.

He conceptualized as 'Satisfying curiosity' and, subsequently, further on in the research process as 'Intellectual satisfaction' the three following items:

'I have always enjoyed learning throughout my whole life'

'I enjoy discovering new ideas, concepts and/or theories'

'I like to step back and gain some hindsight'

He conceptualized as 'Changing career path' and, subsequently, further on in the research process as 'Professional mobility', these other three items:

'I hope the doctorate will allow me to do something [professionally] totally different'

'I trust the doctorate will make me more independent from my current business sector'

'I believe the doctorate will offer me a different option for the last stage of my career'

As you carry on with open coding, fieldnotes help you to begin the conceptualization process while still 'in the field' as you listen and look for the main concern and note indicators of how that concern is processed or resolved. Students often ask about the right way to do fieldnotes, but there is no one right way. Variations on fieldnotes are common to many professions – the proceedings of a business meeting may be captured as minutes, journalists will make notes during interviews, lawyers keep case notes, doctors and nurses observe and make note of a patient's symptoms, etc. Fieldnotes in GT are not intended to serve as detailed evidentiary notes as would be common to the health or legal professions; instead, GT fieldnotes are simply in-the-moment reminders of incidents that may indicate potential concepts. There is no need to try to capture detailed descriptions. You need only capture enough detail about the incidents being shared or observed so that you will be able to later code your notes for those concepts and elaborate your ideas in memos. For instance, when you are interviewing, simply jot down keywords as you listen and complete your fieldnotes as soon as you have an oppor-tunity to code and memo your ideas. Or, when you are developing a questionnaire based on verbatim data and during the statistical analysis, you realize that one of the indicators is pointing to a completely new concept. Or, still, when analyzing quantitative data, when exploratory factor analysis points at an item as double loading on two categories previously identified as different. You can take some brief notes as you go along, until you have time to go back to your qualitative data and investigate further. Waiting too long, however, may mean that you lose some of the insights that triggered the initial note. These fieldnotes about what is really happening in the substantive area – what appears to be the main concern – can then be coded and elaborated through memoing.

Successful open coding will be achieved when the **core category** of your grounded theory has emerged. The core category is the category that keeps recurring in the data and appears to explain significantly how the main concern is processed, man-aged, or resolved.

Selective coding

Once the core category has emerged, coding becomes selective and limited to only those concepts (or variables) that relate to this core category in significant ways (see Box 3.7 for an illustration). During initial open coding, the analyst will have coded many incidents, some of which might not be relevant to the core category: these are eliminated from further analysis as the core category is the guide to moving on with theoretical sampling through further data collection to saturate the core category, its dimensions, and properties. If you are afraid of losing a great incident, idea or concept, you can create a folder named 'after the project' where you will collect all the interesting ideas, codes, concepts and relationships that you had to let go as they were not related to the core category you concentrated on for your dissertation. Then, once your work is completed, you can go back to this folder and write a different theory of your data. It is not uncommon to see several theories emerging from the same set of data as we must remember that the social world is one of complexity with several inherent patterns of social behavior.

All incidents that have been coded are reviewed. Their relevance and relationship to the core category are considered and transcribed through memo writing. When additional data fail to yield any new properties or dimensions of a concept, concepts are considered saturated and set aside while you continue to theoretically sample and saturate the remaining concepts. Theoretical sampling and constant comparison are now only focused on the core category and related concepts; this prevents you from collecting huge amounts of unfocused data that may overwhelm you. If you started with qualitative data, the process of selective coding is sometimes limited by your interpretation of the data and capacity to synthesize parsimoniously all the data obtained. In some instances, this drawback may be considerably lessened by using quantitative data and techniques to help quantify and interpret qualitative results. Conversely, if you started with quantitative data, you might need qualitative data to help you understand and qualify your results to proceed with selective coding. Once you have identified a core category, as well as those concepts that bear some relationship to the core, and you have theoretically sampled to saturate this core and related concepts and you will be ready to begin the process of theoretical coding as the final shaping of your theory.

Box 3.7   Illustration of some selective coding

Once again we use Hendrik's research about business managers engaged in a doctoral program. The main concern of the doctoral program managers that he had interviewed was to understand why successful business managers would engage in pursuit of a doctoral degree. The core category of his work that emerged as answering this question was a two-pronged one: 'self-accomplishment' that included 'personal self-accomplishment' and 'professional self-accomplishment'. He then selectively recoded all relevant open codes around this two-pronged core category. For instance, his open-code/category 'Intellectual satisfaction' was one of the dimensions of 'Personal self-accomplishment', and 'Professional mobility' was one of the dimensions of 'Professional self-accomplishment'.

Theoretical coding

Theoretical coding is undertaken after the core category and related categories have emerged and been fully developed (saturated). It is the final stage of the coding process and helps you shape your theory, i.e. it helps you with the modeling of relationships between and among the core category, and related concepts as an integrated theory. It is at this point that some theorists fail and default through simply offering a conceptual description rather than pressing on through theoretical coding. In classic GT terms, describing is not theorizing: a set of concepts without any interesting relationship between them does not make a classic grounded theory. Theoretical codes conceptualize (i.e. model) how substantive codes relate to each other as propositions (or hypotheses to be verified) to be integrated into a theory. They provide a 'broad picture' – the **pattern** emerging from your data. You may find a dominant theoretical code (e.g. a typology; see Box 3.8) or you might need to consider several theoretical codes. As Glaser has stated, 'life is complex and therefore the analyst may need multiple theoretical codes to formulate his GT' (Glaser, 2005: 45).

Box 3.8   Illustration of theoretical coding

The main theoretical code of Hendrik's research (see Boxes 3.6 and 3.7) was a typology of business managers enrolled in doctoral studies. He found a series of different profiles that depend on the strength of each dimension of his two-pronged core category. These profiles were: the hedonist, the over-achiever, the status-chaser, the ambitious, etc.

When you write your theory, theoretical coding may be expressed implicitly or explicitly: it is emergent and achieved through **theoretical sorting**, i.e. the sorting of accumulated theoretical memos solely by hand and/or with the help of software. Theoretical sorting should always be undertaken with some balance between creativity and reasoning. You have to remain open, even to counterintuitive results or contradictions to existing literature as these could be the main contributions of your work.

At the time when classic GT was first proposed and formalized into a research approach, it was mainly to compensate for the lack of a recognized exploratory research process applied with qualitative data (see Chapter 2). At that time, software development was not as far-reaching as it is today, and GT was mostly used with qualitative data. Some software are now sufficiently advanced to help with theoretical coding of qualitative data (e.g. Mind Manager, QSR*NVIVO, etc.) without jeopardizing the emergence and exploratory quality of these codes. Also, more and more researchers are using mixed (qualitative and quantitative) data while doing GT. Using statistical software with quantitative data to conduct, for instance, cluster analysis and/or partial least squares (PLS) path modeling, both of which are fundamentally exploratory multivariate techniques, can be of great help in highlighting theoretical codes. Thus, we do not eliminate the possibility of developing theoretical codes through theoretical sorting with the help of some software, provided an exploratory approach and discovery stance are always ensured.

Theoretical sorting helps in finding the emergent fit of all ideas into a parsimonious theory of some scope and with no relevant concepts omitted. Sorting can be done through sticky notes or index cards, on a table, on the floor, with the help of mind-mapping or statistical software. Some researchers find that drawing diagrams triggers their creativity and helps them visualize potential ways of theoretically modeling their emerging theories. The best way to 'test' your theoretical codes and the integration and overall shape of your grounded theory is to write the first draft of it, which will eventually become the results section and/or the discussion section of your thesis. You will need to start writing this first draft with a very brief explanation of the context and the main concern, and how the core category works to continuously process or resolve that issue or concern.

The different types of coding to be undertaken while going through the different steps of the classic GT research process, and described in this section, are summarized in Table 3.1. These three types are also illustrated in the GT Tree (see Figure 3.3). This diagram provides an overall and articulated picture of the types of coding applied together with their outcome (main concern, core category, concept, relationships between concepts). In Figure 3.3, the number (1) indicates the use of open coding, (2) the use of selective coding, and (3) the use of theoretical coding.

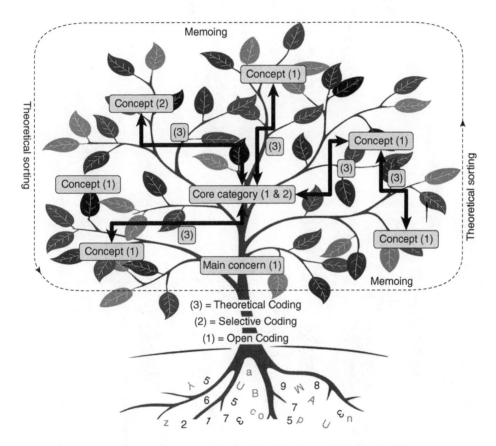

Figure 3.3 The GT Tree - the three types of coding to apply in classic GT

Using software to code data

Regarding quantitative data, and to help you code these data, it is often quite necessary, if not mandatory nowadays, to use one or more of the available statistical software, e.g. R, SPSS, STATA, XLSTAT etc.

To code your qualitative data, you might be tempted to adopt some software developed for qualitative data analysis. While some software like QSR*NVIVO or

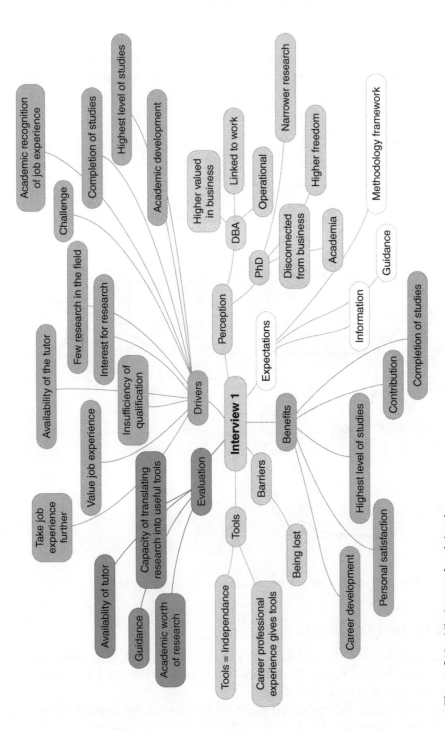

Figure 3.4 Mind-map of an interview

Source: Hendrik Lohse's DBA dissertation, 2018

Atlas.ti are quite compatible with GT, no software will ever do the actual GT coding work for you. This type of software might help you sort, or mine into, your data. They may be useful in 'archiving' coded data, linking memos to incidents in the data as they cumulatively build ideas, but they may also stifle your analytic creativity. The authors of this book find that this type of software is most useful in the final stages of the research when the theory has emerged and the categories/concepts are close to being fully saturated, to help sort all their data towards writing the final draft of their emerging theory.

Some find that mind-mapping software can also be useful to help conceptualization (as an illustration, please see Figure 3.4). Based on the mind-map of the interview that is illustrated in this figure, 'take a job experience further', 'value job experience', 'insufficiency of qualification' were categorized as 'Drivers' in the research from which this diagram is extracted, and that studies drivers and barriers to studying for a DBA (Doctorate in Business Administration).

There is, of course, a learning curve associated with adopting any new software. However, the learning curve associated with this latter intuitive type of software (i.e. mind-mapping) is less time-consuming than the former (qualitative data analysis software).

SUMMARY

In Chapter 3, we detailed the various components of a classic GT approach. More specifically, we described its fundamental principles: emergence and how to avoid 'forcing' concepts to the data; constant comparative analysis and the meaning of 'interchangeability of indicators' when comparing incidents; and theoretical sampling and how it is guided by conceptual emergence and relevance, while limited by the saturation of the concepts. We also highlighted the importance of memoing throughout the GT research process and described the different types of coding required. These include open coding to identify in the data 'incidents' that appear to indicate one or more concepts. The results of open coding are the main concern and the core category. Following open coding and the emergence of the core category, selective coding is initiated to identify concepts related to the core category, its dimensions and properties. The result is the saturation of the core category and its related concepts. Finally, theoretical coding shapes the theory by modelling the relationships between and among the core category and related concepts – the result is the conceptual model of the grounded theory.

4

DOING GT — THE 'FULL PACKAGE'

'In general, the zeal for doing GT, the excitement, the exhilaration, the drive knows no bounds. Many GT researchers love it and devote much of their career life to it.' (Glaser, 1998: 63)

INTRODUCTION

In this chapter, we propose a general outline of the GT research process and its 'tool-box' in seven steps, defined through the outcome of each of these steps:

- Step 1: Finding the main concern.
- Step 2: Finding the core category.
- Step 3: Identifying the concepts related to the core category.
- Step 4: Drafting the rough outline of your theoretical model.
- Step 5: Writing the first draft of your theory.
- Step 6: Integrating your theory with the literature.
- Step 7: Proposing a new theory grounded in data.

After describing in some detail and illustrating the seven-step GT process, we propose some means for you to evaluate the quality of your GT study and answer some questions that are frequently asked by our students while doing GT.

THE SEVEN-STEP GT PROCESS

For each step, we highlight the main question(s) that should guide your actions, the 'tools' to be used for each of these steps, and their outcome.

These seven steps are summarized in Figure 4.1. In this diagram, the boxes with full lines summarize the steps themselves whereas the boxes with dotted lines highlight elements that you have to carry out repeatedly all through the process. The GT research process is not linear. Throughout the entire GT research process, you will keep collecting data, analyzing and constantly comparing these until you reach saturation - i.e. when new data do not highlight any new concepts, properties of or relationships between concepts. You might have to go back to previous steps, and code and recode your data a number of times in an iterative fashion.

During all seven steps of this process, you will write your ideas as they emerge in field-notes to capture what is going on. These fieldnotes are a valuable source of data. You will also write memos to synthesize your fieldnotes and ideas throughout all of the GT research process to integrate and articulate your ideas. These memos are also data and will require regular sorting and grouping like other empirical data. Sorting helps generate the theory and its writing up. When you sort your memos, you will not do so idly. They will have to fit somewhere or be put aside in a 'left out' pile as non-fitting or non-relevant; usually, this pile is small. However, if you find you have a large number of memos in your 'left out' pile, you may need to sort again, write more memos, and possibly even theoretically sample more data to help fit these memos into your overall memo sort. If a memo can fit in several places, it should be placed preferably, and if possible, where it fits best to help the write-up of the emergent theory. Sometimes a memo needs to be separated into two different memos. While relatively rare in our experience, you may also need to duplicate a memo. When described in writing, memo sorting may sound like a tedious process, however it is the complete opposite. As Glaser (1998) states, watching your theory emerge out of your own memos is a time of great excitement and joy!

After describing each of the seven steps of the GT process, we illustrate each of these steps, using as an example the grounded theory of one of our master's students.

Step 1: Finding the main concern

During this first step, the question to ask yourself and aim to answer is, "What is the main concern?" This concern is not your main concern as a researcher, but the main concern of the people you include as the participants to your research. The main concern is their prime motivator, their interest, or their problem that you are going to investigate. You will need to keep collecting data until you find the main concern common to most participants to your research. The purpose of this first step is to find this main concern through the open coding of your data.

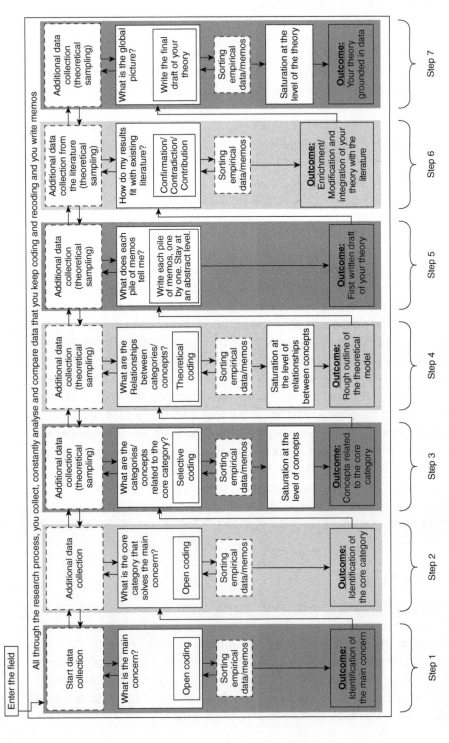

Figure 4.1 The seven steps of the GT research process*

*The boxes with full lines summarize the steps themselves whereas the boxes with dotted lines highlight elements that you have to carry out repeatedly throughout all of the process.

Source: inspired by Nandram et al., 2018

As a grounded theorist you can start by going to the empirical field and collecting data at once through open questions, asking yourself: 'What can I learn about this phenomenon that interests me? What is actually happening in the data that I am collecting, and which are related to this phenomenon? What is the participants' main concern and how do they manage or resolve it?' Even when you believe quantitative data will be useful to help you investigate the phenomenon that interests you, you will often need to collect some qualitative data to identify the participants' main concern.

When undertaking classic GT, you will not need to start with a literature review. You will usually begin your research with a domain or a phenomenon that interests you. Not starting with the literature review allows you to remain 'open' to unexpected incidents and to avoid forcing your study in a given theoretical direction. However, sometimes your university might expect you to start with a literature review. If this is the case, you can review the broad literature in your intended research domain as well as other tangential domains/research fields, at the same time as you start collecting empirical data - all the while keeping a 'mental wall' between the review of the literature and what your data 'tell you'. For example, in Holton (2007) the overall aim of the study was to generate a grounded theory that explained the participation of knowledge professionals in work-related informal activities. To satisfy the dissertation requirements for a literature review, a contextual overview was conducted, highlighting significant issues that impacted upon knowledge-intensive organizational environments including the nature of knowledge work, social and self-organizing aspects of knowledge work, organizational change, the learning organization, workplace motivation, and commitment.

To avoid preconceptions from the literature, it is best to start data collection with no imposed theoretical framework, no defined research questions, and no interview protocols; rather, simply begin with an open mind and one 'grand tour' question, e.g. 'What is it like to be a retail manager?' Do not let yourself reconsider what you find if it contradicts what other researchers have found: such contradictions could indicate the premise of some very interesting results.

At the end of the first step, you will have identified the participants' main concern so you can look for the core category during the next step.

Step 2: Finding the core category

Having found your research participants' main concern, you must now turn to finding out how they address and/or resolve this concern. During this step, you will continue open coding, looking for the core category amongst all other concepts and categories that are emerging from your data. This core category is the category or concept that explains how your study participants manage or process their main concern. To be 'core' the category must appear frequently in your data and account for much of what is happening with regard to the main concern. During this step, keep asking yourself the question: 'What is the category that appears frequently in my data and accounts for much of what is happening with regard to the main concern and that solves/addresses this main concern?'

The core category will relate to several other concepts. It will provide a focus for subsequent theoretical integration through the elaboration of its relationships with other emerging concepts. Indeed, this theoretical integration is the 'prime function' (Glaser, 1978) of the core category, and offers you a way to organize and explain your theory through a pattern or a model centered on this core.

At the end of the second step, you will have identified the core category of your theory. You will be aiming to identify all concepts related to this core category during the next step.

Step 3: Highlighting the concepts related to the core category, its dimensions and properties

Once the core category has emerged, you need to cease open coding and move on to selective coding. The purpose of this step will be to identify all categories/concepts that are related to the core category. Here, you will have to limit your coding to the core category and any concepts that appear to be related in some way to it. You will need to revise, and if need be, recode collected data, and collect additional data.

During this step, you theoretically sample new data slices to build and elaborate your core category and its properties and dimensions. Concepts related to the core category may be its dimensions or properties. Other concepts/variables may be related to the core or linked to it through causal, mediating or moderating relationships. You will need to continue until you feel that you have saturated these concepts, i.e. until no new ideas are emerging regarding your concepts, and you are simply seeing similar indicators over and over, when you collect new data.

Glaser and Strauss speak of data slices as different views or vantage points, and suggest that 'theory generated from just one kind of data never fits, or works as well as theory generated from diverse slices of data on the same category' (1967: 68). By employing a range of data slices, you may discover similarities and differences that can help explain your concepts and their properties in various contexts and under varying conditions, thereby enhancing the conceptual elaboration of the emerging theory.

At the end of the third step, you will have achieved saturation of your core category and related concepts. You will now have the different components/variables of your theory. However, you will not as yet have a clear picture of their relationships. It is, therefore, necessary for you to go up to a further level of abstraction so that you can see the pattern, model or framework that integrates and explains your theory, and start drafting your theoretical model during the next step.

Step 4: Drafting the rough outline of your theoretical model

During this step, through theoretical coding, the relationship(s) between your core category and its related concepts will be emerging. Aim to highlight the rough outline of the conceptual model that is emerging from your data. Explore and look for the relationship(s) between the core category, related concepts, and their properties to discover emerging relationships and obtain the whole picture.

Grounded theories are often modeled as a process or a typology but there are many different ways to model a theory (see Glaser, 1978; Chapter 4) and you should let only the data guide you toward your emerging theoretical model. The questions to ask your-self during this step are: 'How are other categories related to the core category? What type of relationship exists between the core category and the other categories?'

You will code data already collected, theoretically sample further data slices, sort and re-sort your memos, all the while focusing on the theoretical coding of relation-ships between concepts until you reach saturation at the level of relationships, i.e. no new relationship emerges through new data collection, memo sorting and theoretical coding. The sorting and re-sorting of memos is a significant and useful tool for allow-ing the emergence of new theoretical codes, especially when they are not explicitly present in the data – which is often the case.

At the end of step 4, you will have a rough outline of your theoretical model. Having sorted your data and memos throughout each step, you will also have several piles of memos at the end of this step. At this stage, each pile corresponds to a concept or a rela-tionship between concepts. If it helps you, you should be able to summarize the rough outline of your model through a diagram. Some theorists find that diagramming helps them visualize potential ways of theoretically modeling their emerging theories. You should now be ready to start writing the first draft of your theory during the next step.

Step 5: Writing the first draft of your theory

The question to answer during this step is 'What does each pile of memos tell me?'

Once the memos are theoretically sorted, you will be eager to write on paper the theory that you 'see' in your data and able to produce a first rough draft of your conceptual ideas. This first draft is 'a "write up" of piles of ideas [the piles of memos] from theoretical sorting' (Glaser, 1978: 128). You need to write the story told by each pile of memos in simple, conceptual terms. It is 'writing concept to concept relations integrated into a conceptual theory' (Glaser, 2012: 111); it is certainly not like writing fiction. You can start with a very brief explanation of the context and the main con-cern and how the core category works to process or resolve that issue or concern. Hand sorting of memos allows you to see how best to conceptually organize this first draft and assists in writing the theory both conceptually and parsimoniously without reverting to detailed description. Perfection in terms of style, grammar, etc. is not required for this first draft, which is not written in order to please a supervisor. The purpose here is only to put the theory on paper. In turn, this first draft becomes a memo in itself.

Even though Glaser often advises not to voice one's ideas and not to subject them to other people's judgment until the theory has fully emerged, it may be useful and important for you to offer this first draft for your supervisor's feedback as it will help strengthen your results and identify weaknesses. If your supervisor finds your preliminary results interesting, this will provide great encouragement to complete your research project. In any case, proposing first or intermediate drafts of your grounded theory to your supervisor for their perusal and informed comments will help prepare you toward your ultimate purpose of writing your actual thesis, while identifying possible issues.

At the end of step 5, you will have written the first draft of your theory and the time will have come to compare your findings with theories that have been developed by other researchers, and which you will find in the literature.

Step 6: Integrating your theory in the literature

The question to ask yourself during this step is 'How do my results fit with the existing literature?' In classic GT terms, once your core category, related concepts, and relationships have emerged and the first draft of your theory has been written, you will find yourself at the optimal stage at which to start investigating the literature around your core category in depth. This investigation of the literature avoids your 'reinventing the wheel', and rather allows you to integrate what you find in the literature with your results and identify your contribution(s), i.e. what you have found that confirms what had been found before and/or what you have found that is new and different.

How to conduct a literature review is beyond the purpose of this book, but we will only say that a good way to go about it, in line with your GT approach, would be to investigate the literature focusing on your main concern and core category. The challenge here is to make sure all relevant pieces of literature are covered, sometimes reaching outside your field of research. For instance, a core category may have emerged in your research and, while you are unaware of it, may also be related to a discipline and/or research field different from your own. We provide an illustration of this in Box 4.1 below.

Box 4.1   Illustration of a core category anchored to the psychology field, in management research

In Chapter 1, Box 1.3, we mentioned Miriam's research about well-being at work. She conducted her research in a managerial perspective, investigating if there was any possibility for managers to improve employees' well-being at work. After her core category had emerged and she had started drafting her theory, she conducted her literature review. While she found many studies linked to her own research in human resource management, she also discovered a whole research field in psychology, termed 'positive psychology', which fitted her research. Had she not investigated other disciplines beyond management she would have bypassed important results obtained by other researchers. Her review would have been considered incomplete, and more especially as some of her results fitted particularly well with some of the literature in the psychology discipline.

During this step, you will be aiming to find all relevant existing theories that your own emergent theory confirms or contradicts. This will help highlight the academic contributions of your work. By highlighting perspectives that might be different from your own, this might also lead you to enrich and/or slightly readjust your results in order for them to be integrated with existing literature.

Having covered the existing literature, you will be ready to start writing the final draft of your theory during the next step.

Step 7: Proposing a new theory grounded in data

The questions you will aim to answer during this last step are *What is the phenomenon that I have discovered, what is the story that explains it, what has been found before, what have I found and how does it all fit together?*

During this step, you will aim to reach saturation at the level of the theory, i.e. when no new data slices, including theoretical samples from the literature, bring new elements into your theory. Only then will you be able to write the final draft of your thesis, summarizing the theory you found as grounded in your data.

In Box 4.2 we provide an example of a grounded theory extracted from the thesis of one of our master's students with practical illustrations and explanations of all the steps.

Box 4.2   Illustration of the seven-step process (Source: Anouk Vazeux-Blumental's master's thesis, 2018)

Anouk, a French student in a business school, studied 'fast casual' restaurants (i.e. an intermediate type of restaurants between fast food restaurants and casual dining ones) and their key success factors (KSFs). Here is a chronological view of how

(Continued)

(Continued)

she developed her model. This is, of course, a simplified and condensed version of her full thesis (which covers 75 pages), through which we hope to provide a concrete and simple illustration of the seven-step process of GT theory development. The memos were written in French. We have translated the simplified final version of the theory where the different elements are considered together. The process was iterative, and we only provide here the main outcomes of each of the seven steps described in this chapter.

Steps 1 and 2: Finding the main concern and the core category

She found that for these fast casual restaurants, the traditional marketing approach, where the consumer is seen as a target, has been reversed by the consumer. In fact, the consumer is now targeting the fast casual restaurant and is looking for specific, explicit or implicit characteristics. As the resolution of the main concern (i.e. what are the fast casual restaurants' KSFs?) is directly related to the fast casual restaurant itself, the core category has been named 'Becoming the Target'.

When the fast casual restaurant can fit perfectly (i.e. become) the consumer's target, then an important KSF is achieved (main concern).

Steps 3 and 4: Highlighting the main concepts related to the core category and drafting a rough outline of the theoretical model

After identifying the main concern and the core category, Anouk was then able to sort out the characteristics targeted by customers and organize them in her theory (selective and theoretical coding).

The result of open coding and selective coding led to many codes and memos which were subsequently sorted. The illustrations are used here to visually illustrate sorting rather than for their content itself. We show two sortings according to two different views that emerged while sorting. First, Anouk did a sorting of the different elements that explain why fast casual restaurants are preferred to fast food restaurants.

Second, Anouk also sorted the memos according to the KSFs that appear to impact consumer's satisfaction. Please note how the organization is different, even though the code/concepts and memos are from the same data.

After working for four months on the topic, Anouk came up with the following complex diagram (in French) that represents everything she learned from the data analysis. Note that behind each concept or relationship, there are several memos,

Figure 4.2

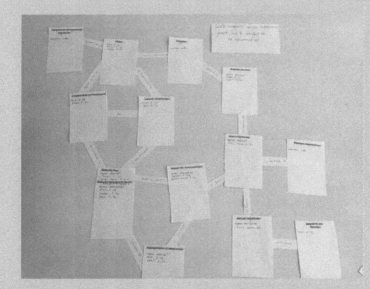

Figure 4.3

codes and data supporting their emergence and relevance. It is interesting to see that in this figure the arrows (i.e. the theoretical codes) have different meanings. Sometimes the arrows are one-sided, and other times they are double-sided. These relationships or theoretical codes emerged from coding the data. For example:

(Continued)

(Continued)

> some arrows are labelled 'criteria' and point to the various criteria related to the quality of the products: (1) freshness of the products, (2) healthy products, (3) dietetic products, etc.;
>
> other arrows are labelled 'requires' such as 'the client requires the restaurant to be extremely clean' or 'the client requires the restaurant to have a specific ambiance and design.'

During this step, theoretical coding of data is carried out and the relationships between the various concepts are explored. Sometimes, there are several types of theoretical codes as in in Anouk's example, while in other works, there is only one main theoretical code. For example, in Grégoire's thesis (briefly described in Box 3.4 in Chapter 3) there are only two theoretical codes (typology of maturity and configuration), which explains how the different types of maturities are integrated into one model, and how they interact with one another in specific configurations.

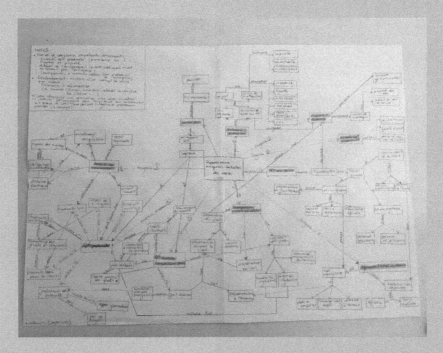

Figure 4.4

Based on this very complex schema, Anouk then highlighted the main concepts/categories that were related to the core category (the big box in the middle). She was then able to conceptualize her theory at a higher level, distinguishing between the explicit and implicit targets.

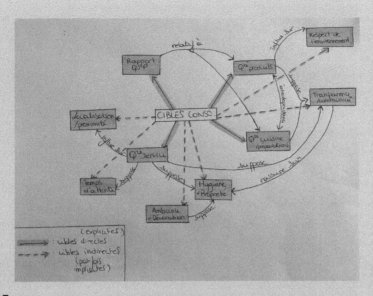

Figure 4.5

After formatting and translating the main concepts, including an additional search toward finding the best name for the core category, the outline for the model can be seen in Figure 4.6.

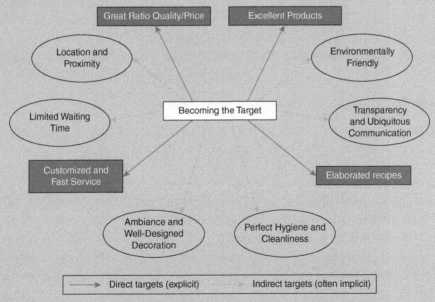

Figure 4.6

(Continued)

(Continued)

Step 5: Writing the first draft of the theory

It is important to note that in her 75-page thesis, the model is thoroughly written up, developed and discussed. Here, we present most of the main outcomes (the 'skeleton') without the 'conceptual meat' that will generate a dense and rich theory.

Step 6: Integrating the theory in the literature

Anouk turned to the literature to enrich the model with concepts that she could have missed. In her case, due to the circumstances of her thesis, she had already conducted an extensive literature review *ex ante*, so a large part of the work was already done, and the core category, luckily for her, was not too far removed from the previous literature she had read. However, she proceeded with further in-depth investigations of the literature, asking marketing professors for references in which the customer targets a product and the supplier becomes the target. Going about her literature review in this way and from this angle, she identified some further recent and relevant literature, which she was able to integrate in her work.

Step 7: Proposing a new theory grounded in data

The finalized and integrated model was presented in her thesis. The examiners – including a professional marketer – strongly encouraged her to publish her results in order to communicate them to a wider audience, as the implications of her work for anyone starting a fast casual restaurant were deemed quite significant.

Assessing the quality of a grounded theory

A grounded theory does not require evidence in the traditional sense of verification. It necessitates only enough 'evidence' to establish a suggestion, to propose a theory, 'not the excessive piling up of evidence to establish a proof' (Glaser & Strauss, 1967: 39–40). However, it also requires careful procedural grounding in data and then conceptual modifications when new data emerge (Glaser, 2003). The methodological procedures that you apply while doing GT incorporate their own mechanisms for theory testing and validation. When doing GT, the search for patterns aggregates incidents in the same way that surveys aggregate people (Glaser, 1998). Thus, concept validation and theoretical integration are essential aspects of theory generation through GT's constant comparison and interchangeability of indicators (Glaser, 1995). This constant grounding keeps the theory close to the data.

Glaser (1978, 1992) proposes four quality criteria for a grounded theory as the end product of a GT approach:

1. *Fit or validity*: The theory must be applicable to and indicated by the data under study. The criterion of fit refers to the validity of the concepts in the theory; in other words, how well they represent the behavior that is being conceptualized.
2. *Workability*: The theory must be transferable within the same substantive area to contexts other than the specific one investigated. Workability refers to the ability of a grounded theory to explain and interpret behavior in a substantive area and to predict future behavior.
3. *Relevance*: The theory must have practical value and be applicable to many situations. Relevance refers to the theory's focus on a core concern or process that emerges in a substantive area and to its being conceptually grounded in data that indicate the significance and relevance of this core concern or process. Grounded theory's relevance is of particular importance in a discipline like business and management where 'the dependent variables are vital, relevant and yield high impact main concerns' (Glaser, 1995: 4).
4. *Modifiability*: You should be able to continue to confront your theory with reality and, if need be, modify it. Modifiability refers to a grounded theory's ability to be continually modified as new data are collected and produce new concepts, properties or dimensions of the theory, thus ensuring its continuing relevance and value to the social world from which it has emerged (Glaser & Strauss, 1967; Glaser, 1978). This continuing openness to being modified is a powerful feature of GT. At a conceptual level, a grounded theory is an abstract of the particulars of a specific substantive case. This means that the theory can be constantly modified as new data, grounded in changing conditions, generate new properties and dimensions to be integrated into the theory. The resultant theory stays alive and relevant through its modifiability.

Furthermore, Glaser and Strauss (1967) highlighted that a 'good' grounded theory should be logical, clear, parsimonious and have density and scope: 'It accounts for as much variation in behaviour in the action scene with as few categories and properties as possible' (Glaser, 1992: 18).

The overall GT research process is summarized in Figure 4.7 and provides an overview of the whole process with its global outcome, i.e. a grounded theory, a theory grounded in empirical data.

ANSWERING SOME FREQUENTLY ASKED QUESTIONS

We could not write about GT without addressing some of the practical challenges you might meet while actually doing GT. We find that the best way to do so is to answer some of the frequently recurring questions that students ask us.

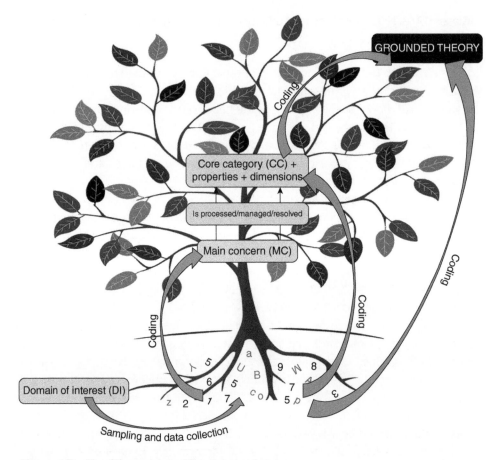

Figure 4.7   The GT process and its global outcome

'How much data should I collect?'

When starting your research you will often need to plan ahead, especially if you do not have a lot of time. Students regularly ask us what quantity of data they should collect, how many interviews they should conduct or how many answers to their survey they should collect. Technically, you should keep collecting data until you reach full saturation at all levels (concepts, relationships, and theory).

If you start or only work with qualitative data, and more particularly if you start a piece of research towards writing a master's thesis, you will not have much time and reaching full saturation at all levels may take more time than you have. You might have to propose a theory which is not fully saturated at all levels. Do not try to hide this. Just mention it at the end of your thesis as a limitation of your work that may be covered in further research. If you use solely quantitative data, for results to have statistical meaning, many supervisors will require that you compute the optimal size of your sample, which will be based on your confidence interval and other statistical criteria. If you use mixed qualitative and quantitative data, the issue is less invasive as each set of data can come as support for the others and there is no general rule: you would have to check with your supervisors as to what they require.

In any case, you should code your data as you collect them and memo throughout all of the research process, as memos are data in themselves and will help you towards conceptualization, recognizing patterns in your data and, ultimately, towards full saturation. Data collection in isolation of coding and memoing often results in more data than needed to reach saturation. This might lead you to unnecessarily collect too much data. Too much data may overwhelm and discourage you and undermine your ability to go beyond descriptive details and conceptualize, while locking you into a state of information overload and confusion. Some amount of confusion is quite normal while doing GT, and you have to be able to tolerate this. However, you must not remain locked into this state. If at any stage you feel you are confused and cannot make sense of your data conceptually, stop collecting further data and take a step back from your research. Go for a walk, have a bath, make dinner ... but do stop, and memo when ideas pop up. Then come back to your data, sort and re-sort your memos in piles, and write what each of these piles of memos tells you, until you get to the 'eureka' moment.

'Should I study the participants' main concern or my own main concern?'

When you start doing GT, during the first step of the research process, you are supposed to identify the participants' main concern, not your main concern as a researcher. However, when you choose to investigate a specific domain of research this usually means it interests you, that you yourself have some interest or concern that you wish to investigate in this domain, and sometimes that you also have had some practical experience around this concern. If this is the case, the easiest way around this issue, and to avoid preconception, is to consider your experience as data. You should discipline yourself and put this experience in writing through auto ethnography - use this as a slice of data (Walsh, 2015b), and collect other data from diverse sources, while remaining open to the fact that what you identified as your main concern and the way you addressed it, is only one possibility and one perspective that might be very different from the perspective of other participants to your research.

'How can I be sure that I am conceptualizing?'

One of the most difficult things to acquire as a novice grounded theorist is the capacity to conceptualize your data. Many who are new to GT will provide detailed and accurate descriptions of their data and the contexts in which those data were collected; however, they stop short of conceptualization. You might start with description but, ultimately, you should conceptualize concepts and the relationships between concepts. For instance, you might note the context of a story told by an interviewee as being a set-up with very hot weather. When you code the verbatim 'the warm sunshine made me feel in great form. I did not think that day about all the issues that were bothering me previously', you might conceptualize it as 'hot weather → positive thinking', which indicates a causal relationship between the weather and the participant's state of mind.

'How should I write what I found?'

The GT research process is a 'messy', iterative process with constant 'comings and goings' between data and theorizing. However, when you write up your theory into a dissertation, you will most probably be expected to follow established norms of writing and tell your story in a linear way: introduction, literature review, methodology, results, discussion, conclusion. If so, your research question - the gap in the literature that you will actually fill with your theory - will have to appear in the introduction even though it most probably emerged at the end of your research work. You will have to indicate that you conducted the literature review *ex post* after your theory emerged, even though you are presenting it *ex ante* in your thesis, so that readers can understand your work more easily. In the discussion, you will have to integrate your theory with the literature you reviewed while highlighting your contributions. In the conclusion of your thesis, you will have to answer the research question you had proposed to address in the introduction, even though this question was not formulated until after your theory had emerged.

'How can I be sure to finish on time?'

The GT process can be a long one as any discovery takes time ... concerning master's students, a master's dissertation is usually written over a few months. This is a very short period to complete a grounded theory and therefore the potential risk is not being able to complete it in due time. In addition, you may have to work with one or two advisors who have not necessarily been trained in GT: this could be another potential risk that your work might be misunderstood. A third challenge will be to demonstrate that your work has been well completed and responds to the criteria of academic validity for a master's dissertation. We have compiled below a checklist of academic challenges and some possible solutions to manage and resolve these:

- *Start coding IMMEDIATELY after the first collection of data.* Do NOT let a day pass. You will be taking the risk of accumulating an excessive amount of data, losing energy and forgetting essential data (e.g. observations, body language) that were not immediately recorded in fieldnotes.
- *Set yourself intermediary targets with deadlines.* Without these, you may lose sight of your work, get bogged down in the data, and not be able to 'get out of the data' (Glaser, 2011). Keep in mind the idea of a readiness moment (Glaser, 2012) to help you monitor for a right time to move on to the next step. The targets can be the various outcomes we described in Chapter 4: Identification of the main concern - Identification of the core category - Identification of the concepts related to the core category - rough outline of the theoretical model - first draft of your theory - enrichment/modification and integration of your theory in the literature - your theory grounded in data.
- *Simply name the emerging patterns.* If you find that conceptualizing is challenging, apply the following instructions from Glaser (2011: 12) : 'Look for interchangeable indicators in the data as it is collected, as it is gathered, while using the constant comparative method [technique]. Once the pattern, latent in the data, is found, and indicators are saturated, name the pattern and conceptualization begins.' Naming a pattern is the key to conceptualizing. Strauss was known to repeat endlessly 'to name is to know...'
- *Do not start with the literature.* This has to be adapted to the rules of your institution and advisor, but it is usually a waste of time and energy, as you may well need to refer to a different stream of literature at the end of the GT process when your theory has finally emerged.
- *Keep energy and time for the literature review and integration of your theory.* This is one of the most exciting parts as you can compare your findings with what other researchers have found. It is also one of the most important parts by which to validate academically your dissertation's findings.

SUMMARY

Chapter 4 allowed us to describe in some detail, and illustrate, the seven steps that are essential to drive towards producing a theory grounded in empirical data:

- Step 1: Finding the main concern.
- Step 2: Finding the core category.
- Step 3: Highlighting the concepts related to the core category, its dimensions and properties.
- Step 4: Drafting the rough outline of your theoretical model.

- Step 5: Writing the first draft of your theory.
- Step 6: Integrating your theory in the literature.
- Step 7: Proposing a new theory grounded in data.

We also provided some means to assess the quality of the resulting theory. These means are fit or validity, workability, relevance and modifiability.

Finally, we answered some frequently asked questions such as 'How much data should I collect?' or 'How can I be sure to finish on time?'

5

EXAMPLES OF GROUNDED THEORIES

'I feel a book coming on!' (Glaser, 1998: 193)

INTRODUCTION

In this chapter, we illustrate how the 'full package' of classic GT, and its seven-step research process (as detailed in Chapter 4), have been applied to three different sub-fields of business and management through three studies. The results from these three GT studies are in three empirical articles, previously published in research journals by the authors of this book. Holton (2007) was published in the *Grounded Theory Review*, a journal created by Barney Glaser specifically to publish empirical articles that use classic GT and/or methodological articles about classic GT. Papers published in this journal focus on presenting the theories themselves as grounded in data, rather than in an elaboration of methodological elements or proofs of the scientific approach of the research: it is taken for granted that the full classic GT package has been applied. Mourmant and Voutsina (2017) and Walsh (2014) were published in broader, more traditional and highly ranked research journals. In these journals, researchers not only have to propose significant theoretical and practical contributions but they also have to bring proof that their research was conducted following established scientific norms.

We specifically chose these three studies because they illustrate applications of classic GT with different types of data: qualitative data (Holton, 2007), qualitative data that have been partially quantified (Mourmant & Voutsina, 2017), and mixed

qualitative and quantitative data (Walsh, 2014). The full text of these three GT studies may be found in the relevant journals. Some methodological elements related to
the first article, which were not included in the published version of it, are provided
here. All methodological elements related to the other two articles, which are summarized here, may be found fully detailed in their corresponding published versions.

For each of these three studies, we provide a brief summary (the abstract) and a
synthesis of the main outcomes of the seven-step process described in Chapter 4.
For each of the three studies, we highlight, their philosophical perspective, their main
components and relevant details related to the GT approach.

HOLTON, J.A. (2007)

Rehumanising knowledge work through fluctuating support networks: a grounded theory study, *The Grounded Theory Review*, 6 (2): 23-46.

Abstract

'Through the basic social structural process of fluctuating support networks,
knowledge workers self-organize to overcome the dehumanizing impact of a
rapidly changing workplace context. Such networks operate outside the formal
organization. They are epiphenomenal – self-emerging, self-organizing, and self-
sustaining. Participation is voluntary and intuitive. The growth of fluctuating
support networks facilitates a rehumanizing process, which serves to counter-
balance the dehumanization that knowledge workers experience in the face of
persistent and unpredictable change. The core variable of the theory, the basic
social psychological process of rehumanizing, is characterized by authenticity,
depth and meaning, recognition and respect, safety and healing and kindred
sharing. Rehumanizing gives meaning to work while sustaining energy and commitment. Fluctuating support network relationships offer members validation
and subtle support. Members pursue shared interests and passions. Activities
are characterized by challenge, experimentation, creativity, and learning. The
resultant sense of achievement renews energy and builds confidence, enhancing commitment and bonding thereby sustaining network engagement.' (p. 23)

Synthesis of the main outcomes

In this study, the domain of interest is the busy life of knowledge professionals. The
main outcomes of Holton (2007) are summarized in Figure 5.1. The main concern
of knowledge workers (population investigated) is the dehumanizing impact of their
workplace context. The core category is rehumanizing and the concepts related to

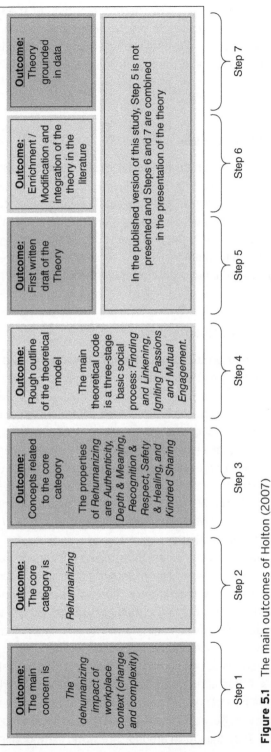

Figure 5.1 The main outcomes of Holton (2007)

the core category are its properties. The rough outline of the theoretical model is provided by the main theoretical code, which is a three-stage basic social process. The first draft of the theory is not presented, which is not surprising in a published study. The integration of the theory in the literature is combined with the presentation of the theory.

Philosophical perspective

This study is positioned within the critical realist paradigm (Bhaskar, 1975) which maintains that social phenomena exist not only in the mind but also in the objective world and that legitimate and reasonably stable relationships can be found among them. These relationships are evidenced in patterns from which the researcher can induce constructs that underlie individual and social life. While not visible, accepted beliefs regarding social phenomena held by those directly involved, render such phenomena real and open to inquiry (Miles & Huberman, 1994: 4).

Main concern and core category

The work of knowledge professionals requires the creative and innovative application of expert knowledge to the solution of organizationally contingent issues. Such issues routinely emerge as a result of persistent change and the application of new technologies and work processes that demand continuous adaptation, learning and collaborative problem solving. The *main concern* that emerged from data was the dehumanizing impact that knowledge professionals experienced in their work and work environments due to the increasing pace and complexity of their workplace context. The author wished to understand, however, what motivates such already very busy knowledge professionals to make frequently unacknowledged investments of extra time and effort in informal relationship building and 'side of the desk' voluntary work-related projects and activities.

The concept of *rehumanizing* emerged as the core category, explaining how knowledge professionals resolve their concerns with the dehumanizing impact of a changing knowledge workplace – how they restore the human dimension in their work relationships and working environments. Dehumanization occurs in the bureaucratic knowledge workplaces where constant information and technological change reduces job security, increases workloads and destabilizes work groups. To ward off dehumanization, knowledge professionals connect for support and survival through the social structural process of fluctuating support networks. These networks form everywhere knowledge professionals connect. These networks may be internal or external to the workplace environment. Networks form at the office, in coffee shops, on the golf course, at the gym or pub. They may form around core work, extra duties, special projects or shared interests. Fluctuating support networks serve as a means through which knowl-edge workers can rehumanize their work and their work environments. Rehumanizing gives meaning to their work while sustaining energy and commitment. Rehumanizing is characterized by the properties of authenticity, depth and meaning, recognition and respect, safety and healing and kindred sharing.

Data collected

The study used solely qualitative data and techniques. In summary, 61 individu-als participated in the study; 27 through personal interviews with an additional 34 individuals participating in focus group sessions that occurred during two retreats. While initially interviews were audio recorded, as the study progressed, these data sources were augmented with additional data from participant observa-tions and serendipitous access to research participants through chance encounters and casual conversations rather than sole reliance on the pre-arranged interviews. Fieldnotes captured during and immediately after these spontaneous opportunities became additional data for analysis. Accordingly, the significance of audio recording and transcribing interviews lessened in value as the author increased her focus on in-the-moment data capturing and conceptualization. The full and detailed account-ing required of more structured interviews became tedious, time-consuming and redundant compared to the speed and pithy relevance of spontaneous data capture (Glaser, 1998: 108-9).

The three main elements: emergence, constant comparative analysis, and theoretical sampling

The participants in the study were knowledge professionals and managers in a range of organizations. The author was interested in discovering what motivates knowledge professionals to participate voluntarily in informal work-related relationships variously described as networks, communities, associations and 'extramural' project teams. In the interviews, rather than launching into a long preamble about her research inter-ests, the author simply asked participants to tell her about their jobs. She listened for what they wanted to tell her. Interviewees voiced concerns about organizational change and the pace of change. She jotted down keywords and phrases during each conversation (e.g. *'fragmented knowledge pockets'*, *'structures eroding'*, *'people marginalized'*, *'how to free people up, opening them up to possibility'*). Her fieldnotes revealed that what these knowledge professionals wanted to talk about wasn't what she had thought she would be researching, but she trusted the process and coded her fieldnotes and memoed. Despite struggling to let go of preconceived ideas and simply trust what was emerging from the data, she continued collecting and coding data:

the main concern - the dehumanizing impact of a changing workplace context - did emerge over and over.

Using the process of constant comparative analysis, the author coded and compared incidents in the data; first open coding until the main concern and core category had been established, then selectively coding for indicators of the core category and what appeared to be related concepts. Initially, incidents are compared to other incidents to generate conceptual codes. Additional incidents are then compared to the generated concepts to further define conceptual properties and dimensions. Each concept earns its way into the theory through constant comparison and the interchangeability of indicators to theoretical saturation. As an example, *authenticity* emerged as a concept that appeared to be related to the core category of *rehumanizing* and in further theoretical sampling and coding of fieldnotes, the author noted several indicators that she conceptualized to further elaborate and theoretically saturate her concept of authenticity including: *'how important it is to give people a voice', 'An experience that allowed me to grow so much as a person', 'We were able to speak very frankly', 'quiet voices ... authentic voices in organizations rather than corporate voices', 'a place where egos and agendas don't seem to get in the way of genuine dialogue and caring for one another', 'a place where she found like minds ... authentic connection', 'getting to really know others .... Building connections', 'corporate relationships are not authentic. They are transactional/ power related ... Where do we find the experience of being ourselves in organizations? Where do we learn to be human?', 'having a chance to be heard, to share with others who understand, who they can trust to help and to hold confidences.'*

Continued theoretical sampling further elaborated the concept. For example, openness and honesty, trust, sharing, being heard, safety, and power balance were all indicators of the property of authenticity.

On memoing

The author wrote memos to conceptually elaborate her ideas - memos such as the following.

The prevalence of the 'machine' metaphor in organizations has dehumanized work environments. Many workers actually begin to view themselves as 'cogs' in a wheel and begin to respond accordingly with automatic, mindless behaviours that further disconnect them from their work. As one interviewee said: 'It appears that the corporate model that most of us work in now squeezes out our humanity. We develop machine relationships - even odd corporate voices ... a manner of speaking a "dead sound" where our real personality has been excluded as has emotion and feeling.' Another interviewee commented: 'This machine world is causing us to become ill and depressed ... We act in this impersonal and unreal way in our whole lives. We even act like this to our-selves and no longer have a real relationship with ourselves. How can we learn and experience being human again? What is the essence of being human? It is surely to hear our real voice.'

The author proceeded to compare *authenticity* with other concepts that were emerging, writing memos about the relationships that linked and integrated these concepts and eventually, through hand sorting of memos, authenticity would emerge as a property of the core category, *rehumanizing knowledge work*, along with the properties of *depth and meaning, recognition and respect, safety and healing* and *kindred sharing*; all were theoretically sampled in relation to the core category of *rehumanizing*.

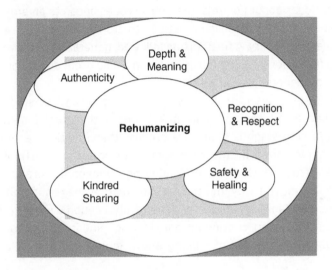

Figure 5.2   The core category and its properties

The model in Figure 5.2 illustrates the conceptual properties of the core category, rehumanizing.

Coding and theoretical saturation

The concept of a *changing knowledge workplace* emerged early in the data collection and analysis process as a significant concern of the research participants. Through constant comparison of data, 51 indicators of the concept were coded to achieve theoretical saturation. Similarly, coding and constant comparison yielded 30 indica-tors of the concept of *authenticity*, 31 indicators of the concept *coping with change*, 58 indicators of the concept *likening*, 62 indicators of *kindred sharing*, 37 indicators of *rehumanizing*, and 58 indicators of *igniting passions*. The number of indicators per category is not as significant as the requirement to sample sufficiently to achieve theoretical saturation. The important thing is that each concept earns relevance in relation to the theory, its relevance theoretically sampled for and sufficiently validated through constant comparison and interchangeable indicators to theoretical saturation.

Outline of the theoretical model

Having achieved theoretical saturation of the core category and related concepts, the author proceeded to review, hand sort and integrate her memos about the core category, rehumanizing, and those concepts that related to the core category. Through sorting memos, ideas about potential theoretical codes began to emerge. Theoretical codes suggest an abstract modeling of latent structural patterns that integrate and explain the emerging theory. A final sorting followed, generating a theoretical outline, or conceptual framework, for the full articulation of the grounded theory through an integrated set of theoretical propositions.

Rehumanizing employs as its primary theoretical code a three-stage basic social process: *Finding and Likening, Igniting Passions* and *Mutual Engagement*. The *Finding and Likening* stage is a subcore process that functions as an amplifying causal loop characterized by the development of an altruistic atmosphere, connectedness, and trust. As altruistic atmosphering, connectedness and trust build or amplify, members move easily into the second stage of the rehumanizing process. This second stage – *Igniting Passions* – is the catalytic middle stage that facilitates the symbiotic relationship, continuous amplification and interdependent functioning of the subcore processes of *Finding and Likening* and *Mutual Engagement*.

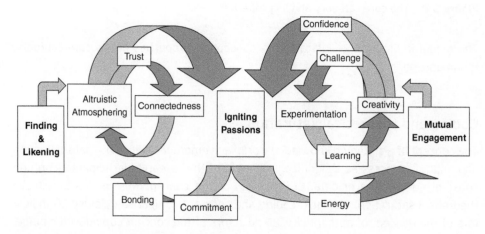

Figure 5.3 A three-stage basic social process

The dynamic capacity of this median stage sustains the overall rehumanizing process by continuously generating confidence, energy, commitment, and bonding among network members. The *Mutual Engagement* stage is another subcore process that also functions as an amplifying causal loop. The *Mutual Engagement* stage is characterized by creativity, challenge, experimentation, and learning. Figure 5.3 models the theoretical coding of the three-stage basic social process with its dynamic amplifying causal loops.

The rehumanizing process begins through a subprocess of finding and likening in which knowledge professionals spark a connection of support, mutual trust and working together outside the confines and control of the formal organization. Once initiated through likening, the rehumanizing process grows and endures as workers build trust and establish a sense of connectedness. The rehumanizing process is characterized by authenticity, depth and meaning, recognition and respect, safety and healing and kindred sharing. Likening reignites the passion that knowledge professionals describe as lost to the dehumanizing effects of the knowledge workplace. It encourages mutual engagement, opening them up to creativity, challenge, experimentation and learning. Rehumanizing builds confidence and commitment. It energizes and bonds workers thereby amplifying and sustaining the rehumanizing process.

Type of theory produced

Holton (2007) proposes a type 2 theory (i.e. an explanation) as to how knowledge professionals self-organize through fluctuating support networks to overcome the dehumanizing impact of a rapidly changing workplace context. GT is particularly well suited for exploration of the amorphous nature of emergent and informal organizational entities. The theory's core category of rehumanizing could be further developed as a formal grounded theory through theoretically sampling for indicators of rehumanizing in various aspects of life, e.g. the slow food and local food movements, palliative care, mindfulness practices, responsible eco-tourism, etc.

MOURMANT, G. & VOUTSINA, K. (2017)

Awakening the dormant dream: the concept of entrepreneurial mind-shifts, *ACM SIGMIS Database: the DATABASE for Advances in Information Systems*, 48(3): 110-37.

Abstract

'This paper addresses an under-investigated thematic area of Information Technology (IT) personnel turnover literature: IT Entrepreneurial Turnover. It introduces the concept of entrepreneurial mind-shift in order to shed light on the conditions that influence turnover behavior for nascent IT entrepreneurs. The study follows a grounded theory methodological approach and utilizes two different sets of data. The first dataset comes from interviews with 62 IT entrepreneurs, and the second comes from the quotes of over 200 famous authors/entrepreneurs. The analysis of data revealed the types of perceptual shifts IT professionals experience when they realize that they are ready to quit their salaried job and start a new business. The results of the study show that after certain types of "disrupting events" or the gradual completion of a phase, nascent entrepreneurs start perceiving things through a new lens. In their eyes, the creation of a new venture seemed more feasible than ever before. The introduction of the entrepreneurial mind-shift construct has implications for both research and practice. First, it enriches the stream of literature that brings the concepts of IT personnel turnover and entrepreneurship together. Second, it is a practical tool for all stakeholders involved in the IT Entrepreneurial Turnover process.' (Mourmant & Voutsina, 2017: 110)

Synthesis of the main outcomes

In this study, the domain of interest is the transition from IT employee to IT entrepreneur. The main outcomes of Mourmant and Voutsina (2017) are summarized in Figure 5.4. The main concern of nascent IT entrepreneurs (investigated population) is how to make the transition from being an employee to becoming an entrepreneur. The core category that addresses this main concern is entrepreneurial mind-shifts. The main concepts related to the core category are the different types of entrepreneurial mind-shifts. The rough outline of the theoretical model is provided by the main theoretical code, which is a typology of entrepreneurial mind-shifts. The first draft of the theory is not presented, which is not surprising in a published study. The integration of the theory in the literature is combined with the presentation of the theory.

Main concern and core category

The *main concern* of the (future) IT entrepreneurs is how to make the transition from being an employee to becoming an entrepreneur. The *core category* that explains how a would-be entrepreneur is brought to the decision of becoming an entrepreneur is entrepreneurial mind-shift. The authors identify nine types of entrepreneurial mind-shift. For each entrepreneurial mind-shift, they 'highlight the transition from a "negative state/inhibitor/decelerator" toward a "positive state/enabler/accelerator" to entrepreneurship' (Mourmant & Voutsina, 2017: 116-17).

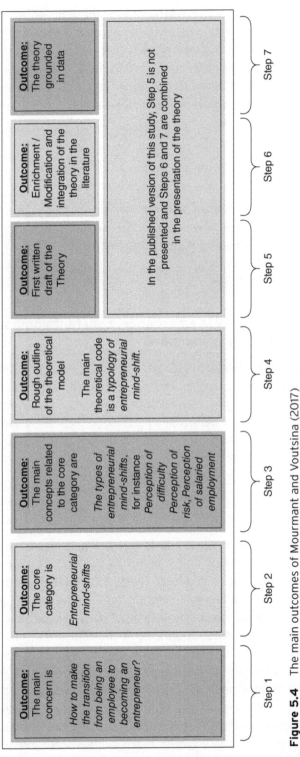

Figure 5.4 The main outcomes of Mourmant and Voutsina (2017)

This study was developed from Gaetan Mourmant's PhD work. From this PhD, two other grounded theories emerged, involving core categories such as readiness to quit (Mourmant et al., 2009) or entrepreneurial epiphany (Mourmant & Voutsina, 2010). The concept of entrepreneurial mind-shift emerged as a third additional core category. In a way, Mourmant and Voutsina (2017) is a spin-off of the initial grounded theory, and a good example of how several theories can emerge from the same set of data.

Data collected

This study uses solely qualitative data: secondary data (quotes from famous people) and primary data (interviews). Two types of data were therefore eventually collected: (i) longitudinal and retrospective interviews with entrepreneurs, and (ii) famous quotes recommended by entrepreneurs.

The three main elements: emergence, constant comparative analysis, and theoretical sampling

Regarding constant comparison analysis, while comparing the famous quotes one with another, it rapidly became clear that a large majority of these were referring to a state of mind before and after. This led to the emergence of the idea of a mind-shift. From there, additional data were collected through theoretical sampling to explore all the types of entrepreneurial mind-shifts that were found not only in the famous quotes, but also in the interviews.

Coding

Here are examples of codes: if you compare the two quotes 'find a job you love and you'll never work a day in your life' (Confucius) to 'Don't sit down and wait for the opportunities to come. Get up and make them!' (C.J. Walker), you should clearly see a before (painful work/waiting for opportunities) and an after (a job you love and no pain/creating opportunities). Interesting constant comparisons were also made between interviews and famous quotes, e.g. if you compare this famous quote – 'I'm convinced that about half of what separates the successful entrepreneurs from the non-successful ones is pure perseverance' (Steve Jobs) – with the interview quote – 'They didn't like to work, and I got fed up. And I just made the decision that I could work as hard as I know how and that I could do it for myself. And so, I quit.' – both of these illustrate the same mind-shift, but one is very general and could be applied everywhere, while the other is very specific to the context of the individual.

Some examples of qualitative data collected towards illustrating dimensions and properties of entrepreneurial mind-shifts are as follows:

- From 'I am fairly paid as an IT employee' to 'I am not paid enough for my level of competency": this was coded and conceptualized as 'entrepreneurial mind-shift related to the perception of salaried employment'.
- From 'I like working for someone or for a company' to 'I don't like working for someone else anymore': this was also coded and conceptualized as 'entrepreneurial mind-shift related to the perception of salaried employment'.
- Famous quote: 'The way to get started is to quit talking and begin doing' (Walt Disney). This quote was coded and conceptualized as 'entrepreneurial mind-shift from procrastination to urgency of action'.

Some of the open codes in this article for the entrepreneurial mind-shift are: 'I think that being an entrepreneur is risky', coded as 'a state of mind before the shock' and 'My employer can fire me anytime he wants', coded as 'a state of mind after the shock'. The pattern formed by these two codes was coded as an 'entrepreneurial mind-shift'. In this context, the shock generating the entrepreneurial mind-shift is illustrated by the following verbatim: 'Five senior IT consultants just got fired following a merger.'

Different types of entrepreneurial mind-shift emerged as we coded. We will consider an example related to risk aversion and risk tolerance: 'I think that being an entrepreneur is risky' was open coded as 'risk aversion', and 'My employer can fire me anytime he wants' was open coded as 'risk tolerance' (in this economy, being an entrepreneur may be perceived as less risky than salaried employment). The pattern formed by these two codes was coded as one of the nine types of entrepreneurial mind-shift: 'perception of risk'.

Quantifying

Some of the qualitative data were coded towards quantifying some of the results and transformed into a graphical representation (radar diagrams) for better readability, easier interpretation and better understanding of these results. To do so, quantitative techniques were applied to qualitative data: qualitative results were quantified. This allowed us to make a series of six charts. By showing a specific case (Stephen), we were able to map the relevant entrepreneurial mind-shifts and refine their theory. In Table 5.1 you will find the first and final charts that show the evolution of the entrepreneur after he spotted an opportunity, realized his job could be replaced by technology, received the emotional and financial support of his dad, and weighed the pros and cons of being a salaried employee. Interestingly, some of the entrepreneurial mind-shifts were not triggered. For instance, his perception of entrepreneurship-related skills was very low, hence he started with partners.

Saturation

At a point during the collection and coding of famous quotes and entrepreneurial mind-shifts, no new types of entrepreneurial mind-shifts emerged from new slices of data, and we considered that we were theoretically saturated with nine types of entrepreneurial mind-shift. Note that our domain of interest was the transition from IT employee to IT entrepreneurs, so there was a conscious choice to delimit the data collection to this population. If we had considered other domains of interest such as the transition from student to social entrepreneur, we would probably have seen additional types of entrepreneurial mind-shift. These would be useful studies if we were to develop a more formal theory of entrepreneurial mind-shift.

Outline of the theoretical model

The theoretical code obtained from theoretical coding is a typology of entrepreneurial mind-shifts, explaining the transition from IT employee to entrepreneur. Nine types of entrepreneurial mind-shift emerged from our data. Each type of entrepreneurial mind-shift refers to a specific shift in the way the IT professional thought about a notion/concept or a domain of activity which was directly or indirectly related to her decision to quit her job and start a company. For each of these nine types, we highlight the transition from a negative state/inhibitor/decelerator toward a positive state/enabler/accelerator to entrepreneurship. This is summarized in Table 5.1.

Table 5.1 Mind-shifts, inhibitors, and accelerators

Mind-Shift	Inhibitor	Accelerator
Perception of salaried employment	From salaried employment as a bargain	To salaried employment as a rip-off
Perception of difficulty	From difficulty as an insurmountable problem	To difficulty as an interesting challenge
Perception of procrastination	From procrastination	To urgency of action
Perception of risk	From risk aversion	To risk tolerance and acceptance of risk as an inherent part of the entrepreneurial process
Desire for entrepreneurship	From a latent, non-sufficiently activated desire	To a burning desire
Perception of Entrepreneurship-Related Skills	From a perceived lack of entrepreneurship-related skills	To perceived adequacy of entrepreneurship-related skills
Passion	From a lack of awareness about passion	To the discovery of passion

Mind-Shift	Inhibitor	Accelerator
Opportunities	From no perceived opportunity	To a large spectrum of opportunities
Broader perspectives	From a lack of greater goal in life	To the formulation of a greater goal in life, of which entrepreneurship is an important part

Source: Mourmant & Voutsina, 2017: 118

Further analysis helped us to illustrate our findings with a radar chart depicting the evolution of our participants' entrepreneurial mind-shifts. Table 5.2 summarizes one of our participants' (Stephen's) entrepreneurial mind-shift.

Table 5.2   Stephen's entrepreneurial mind-shifts

- **Before the shifts,** Stephen is an entrepreneur, who was previously employed in a top consulting firm. We describe here his mind-shifts and their influence on his decision to start a business.

- The scale represents the level of shift. Below is the situation prior to the shifts: Difficulty to start a business is perceived as average; risk of starting a business is perceived as high; salaried employment is perceived as a good thing; Stephen perceives that he does not have the skills required to be an entrepreneur, and no opportunities are perceived.

- **Final shift:** After several shifts (e.g. opportunity, risk), the differences between employment and entrepreneurship are finally weighed.

- *'My father worked 40 years for a very large company, and I saw that he really missed out on some opportunities. There are certain things when you work for someone else that you give up. If they want to move you and your family, they do so. If they want to pass you up for a promotion that you really deserved for some other reason, they can do so.*

- *I sensed that I wanted to have more control. However, I knew that it also would be hard. I don't think I was delusional that it would just be easy. But that's where the drive is'.*

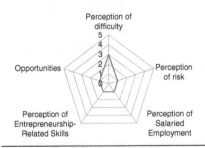
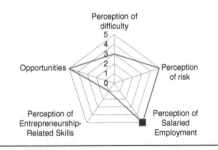

Source: adapted from Mourmant & Voutsina, 2017: 122

Type of theory produced

This study proposes a type 4 substantive theory. As explained in Chapter 2, a type 4 theory for explanation and prediction answers the questions 'What is, how, why, when, where and what will be?'. We also found some elements of a type 5 theory that provides prescriptions and answers the question 'How to do?' For instance, a shock is a potential predictor of an entrepreneurial mind-shift (predictive theory).

With knowledge of the types of entrepreneurial mind-shift, a future entrepreneur can voluntarily create a situation of shock (e.g. taking a measured risk) to trigger a specific entrepreneurial mind-shift (prescriptive theory). For example, an IT programmer can take on the task of selling some software to a client, and being shocked with her success, hence experiencing an entrepreneurial mind-shift in her perception of entrepreneurial related skills – in this case marketing, sales, and risk taking.

WALSH, I. (2014)

A strategic path to study IT use through users' IT culture and IT needs: a mixed-method grounded theory, *Journal of Strategic Information Systems*, 23(2): 146-73.

Abstract

'We consider recent research in IS, as well as recent advances in the fields of psychology and sociology. As an alternative to existing models, we propose a new strategic path to study IT use through users' IT culture and IT needs. Our contributions are (1) theoretical: we investigate the predictive value for IT usage of several new constructs and show that both expectancy-based and needs-based theories of motivation should be taken into account in acceptance models, (2) methodological: we adopt an exploratory, mixed-method, grounded theory approach and use both quantitative and qualitative data and methodology, an unusual approach in IS research that allows new perspectives, and (3) practical: our results highlight the fact that highly IT-acculturated users may hinder (rather than facilitate) new-IT acceptance if their situational IT needs are ignored. Therefore, when the strategic decision of implementing new IT is made, managerial attention must be focused on these users in order to drive toward the alignment of their IT needs and managerially-perceived organizational IT needs.' (Walsh, 2014: 146)

Synthesis of the main outcomes

In this study, the domain of interest is the acceptance and use of new information technologies (IT). IT usage is already very well covered in the literature and the Technology Acceptance Model (TAM) had been used and verified many times. However, this article aims to take a new approach to IT usage through under-investigated constructs (IT needs). The article proves that the TAM is not always verified and proposes a new path to study – explain and predict IT usage (rupture theorizing). The main outcomes from Walsh (2014) are summarized in Figure 5.5. The *main concern* of managers in firms that invest in new and expensive IT is to predict the utilization of these new IT by employees, and whether employees are actually going to use them. The *core category* that explains IT utilization is IT needs, as perceived by users. The main concepts

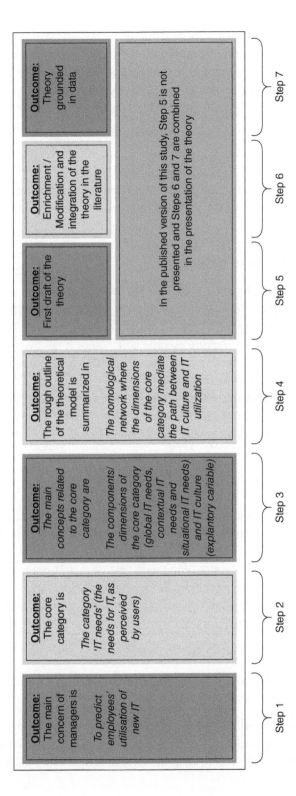

Figure 5.5 The main outcomes of paper 3

related to this core category are its dimensions (global, contextual and situational IT needs), and IT culture. The rough outline of the theory is summarized in the nomological network of constructs proposed in this study. The first draft of the theory is not presented, which is not surprising in a published study. The integration of the theory in the literature is combined with its presentation throughout all of the article.

Philosophical perspective

The philosophical perspective adopted in this study (critical realism) has been previously described in Box 2.2 (Chapter 2) of this book and welcomes any type of data.

Main concern and core category

The main concern of managers is to be able to predict utilization of new IT by employees and allow in firms for different usages of IT by different people. In a previous grounded theory, we had found that IT usage had been strongly linked to IT users' digital culture (IT culture). IT culture was the core category of this previous grounded theory (Walsh et al., 2010). However, the concept 'IT needs' (the need for IT perceived by users) was an unsaturated concept and another core category that needed investigation. It was investigated in this article and emerged as the core category that mediated the path between IT culture and IT utilization. The core category 'IT needs' includes global IT needs, contextual IT needs, and situational IT needs.

Data collected

This article first uses secondary qualitative data (from the 2010 study); primary quantitative data slices were then added as well as qualitative data slices. The last slices of qualitative data were used to qualify the quantitative results, help with the selective coding of all data, and make sense of the quantitative results obtained. All qualitative data were collected through interviews and participant observation, and the quantitative data were collected through two surveys – one administered to students and one administered to professors.

The three main elements: emergence, theoretical sampling, and constant comparative analysis

Emergence is obviously witnessed by the following excerpts: 'three types of IT needs (global, contextual and situational) emerge, as perceived by users' (Walsh, 2014: 149); 'When we collected primary data (quantitative and/or qualitative), we did so as we needed them to move the <u>emerging</u> theory forward' (Walsh, 2014: 150); 'Qualitative data were collected when we needed rich description of the <u>emerging</u> relationships between concepts' (Walsh, 2014: 150). One good example of emergence and of the importance of remaining open to what data tell you is described in this study in the subsection 'Ambassador or Nemesis" of the Discussion part: that two important results which emerged from our data were counterintuitive and could not have been explained otherwise.

Another example of exploration and emergence in this study is highlighted by the fact that 'we ran an exploratory factor analysis'[1] (Walsh, 2014: 168) (and not a confirmatory factor analysis as could have been done): when you do GT, one of the 'musts' is to remain in an exploratory stance regardless of your philosophical stance. If you use confirmatory factor analysis, this means that, based on previous existing theories, you lay down a hypothesis related to the number of factors you are going to find and enter this number in the statistical software used. When you use exploratory factor analysis, you do not presuppose or enter in the software the number of factors and let the data dictate to the software the number of factors that best fits the data.

Concerning the theoretical sampling, the previous grounded typological work, which highlighted users' IT culture (Walsh et al., 2010), is used in this study to guide the theoretical sampling of participants to collect qualitative data. People that fitted some of the IT culture ideal types highlighted in this previous work were preselected. People finally selected to be interviewed were those whose IT culture profile could be identified with sufficient precision, and who were different in terms of age, nationality, and background to allow for different perspectives and because we wished our results to be generalizable to any type of population.

Finally, quantitative and qualitative investigations and analyses are done simultaneously, while taking into account all data as one set, and constantly comparing and analyzing all data as they were collected (constant comparative analysis). It is also clearly stipulated that 'only the final models that emerged from and were congruent with our whole data set' (Walsh, 2014: 151) were provided in the results section.

Coding

Example of open coding: the three verbatims 'I need Moodle to do some of my tasks as a student in X school', 'Some of my tasks as a student in X school necessitate the use of Moodle' and 'For some of my tasks as a student in X school, I need to use Moodle' (Walsh, 2014: 167) were all open-coded as 'situational IT needs' (Task-related IT needs perceived by users in a specific situation and context). The quantitative data

---

[1]Factor analysis helps transform statistical data into linear combinations of independent variables called 'factors'.

related to this concept and collected through answers to two surveys were statistically analyzed and coded with the help of exploratory factor analysis.

In this study, some examples of selective codes related to the core category are the three IT needs constructs that were highlighted: global IT needs, contextual IT needs, and situational IT needs. In the previous study (Walsh et al., 2010), these three constructs were dimensions of the same construct IT needs, which was itself a dimension of the IT culture construct. Using IT needs as the core category in this study allowed us to better saturate it, and show that there were, in fact, three distinct IT needs constructs (global, contextual and situational) that were not part of the IT culture construct, and that they were mediators of the path between IT culture and IT utilization. This also shows that a grounded theory is always a work in progress: it may be modified as you add further data slices, towards formalization of the theory.

The theoretical codes in this study were obtained through hand sorting of qualitative data on a table and with the help of statistical software for quantitative data, for instance POSITION → CONITNEE (the position held by an individual has a significant impact on their contextual IT needs); GLOBITNEE → SITITNEE (the global IT needs perceived by an individual have a significant impact on their situational IT needs); SITITNEE → UTILIZATION (the situational IT needs for some given software perceived by an individual have a significant impact on their utilization of this software).

Saturation at the level of concepts and relationships

Saturation at the level of the concepts/constructs was ensured through exploratory factor analyses of quantitative data, assessment of Cronbach's alphas for all reflective constructs, and various other mathematical validity measures, e.g. variance inflation factors (VIFs). Saturation at the level of the relationships between concepts/constructs was ensured through the comparison and analysis of both our qualitative data (through qualitative theoretical codes) and quantitative data (with the help of partial least squares path modeling and statistical indicators, e.g. the standardized coefficients β of the investigated paths, which indicate the strength of the relationships between each pair of variables, or the R^2 values for each variable, which indicate how much of its variance is explained by its antecedents). Both sets of data were essential to finalize and understand these relationships: see for instance the Ambassador versus Nemesis phenomenon, highlighted in the discussion section of this study; it explains why some users who perceived high global IT needs, also perceived low situational IT needs in the population of professors and more particularly IS professors. This was so because they were consulted, as IS experts, about the platform they were supposed to use, but their opinions and advice were not taken into account. Hence, instead of being valuable ambassadors promoting the new software (as could have been expected from IS professors), and as a revenge for not being listened to, they became the implemented software's worst enemy, its 'nemesis' (Nemesis is the goddess of vengeance in Greek mythology).

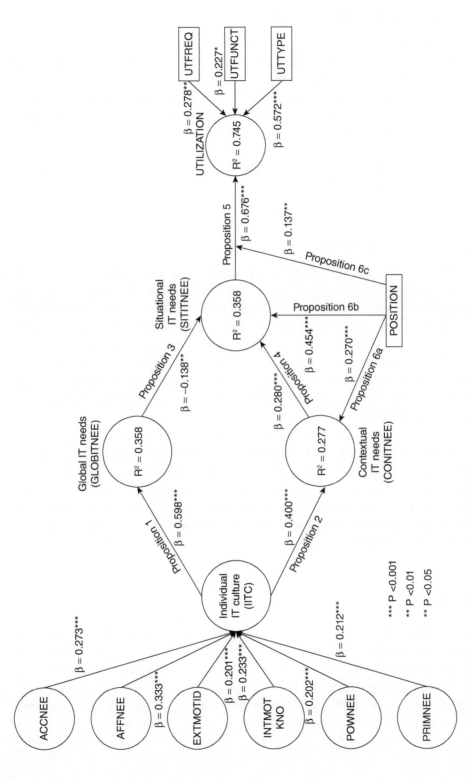

Figure 5.6 Modeling the theory[2] (Walsh, 2014: 154)

---

[2]In this diagram, p is the probability that the hypothesis underlying a path might not be verified.

Outline of the theoretical model

The outline of the theoretical model highlighted by this article is summarized in Figure 5.6 which shows the nomological network (the network of paths between concepts/variables that are verified) that is proposed in the article and includes many different causal paths. A user's Individual IT culture (IITC) does explain her utilization of the IT platform (Utilization) investigated, but through the mediating influence of the user's global, contextual and situational IT needs (GLOBITNEE, CONITNEE, SITITNEE). The position (POSITION) held by the user influences her contextual and situational IT needs and moderates the influence of her situational IT needs on her utilization of the platform.

Type of theory produced

This study proposes a *type 4 theory* (i.e. a theory for explanation and prediction that answers the questions 'What is, how, why, when, where and what will be?' (see Chapter 2), to explain why highly IT-acculturated users may hinder (rather than facilitate) new-IT acceptance if their situational IT needs are ignored and predict IT usage through IT needs. In this study a previous substantive grounded theory already published separately (Walsh et al., 2010) and its core category (the IT culture construct). That first study theorized on a typology of IT users and on the path between IT culture and IT usage. Walsh (2014) refined the theorization on IT needs constructs and the investigated paths.

Some relationships were investigated and confirmed through quantitative techniques with our substantive quantitative dataset, but we did not retain nor report on them as they did not make sense in our complete dataset. Conversely, some other relationships that were not completely confirmed through our quantitative data are discussed, as – from information obtained through our qualitative dataset – they could be important for further research in other substantive areas with different, and less specific, targeted sampling.

SUMMARY

In this chapter we provided three extensive examples of classic GT: the first one using solely qualitative data; the second one using partly quantified qualitative data; and the last one using mixed qualitative and quantitative data. For each example, we detailed how the seven-step GT research process was applied. This is an excellent opportunity to show the diversity of grounded theories. In Figures 5.7 to 5.9 you will find a summary of the main outcomes.

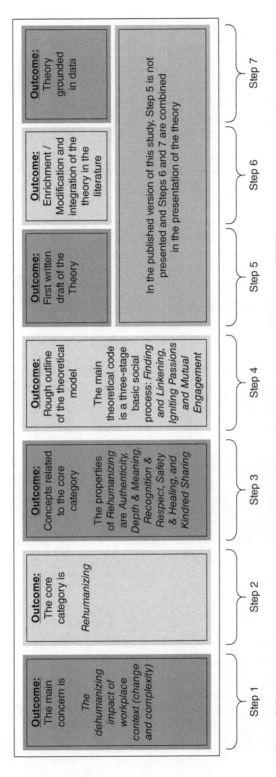

Figure 5.7 Rehumanizing knowledge work through fluctuating support networks (Holton, 2007)

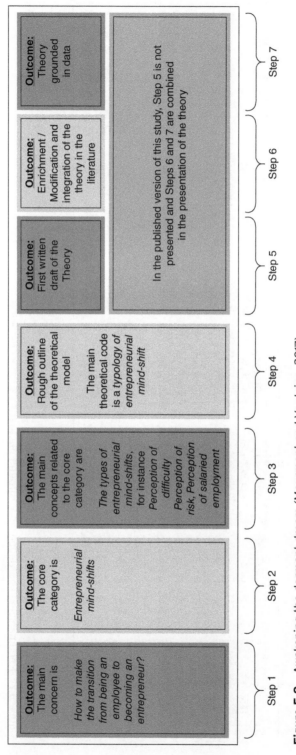

Outcome:
The main concern is

How to make the transition from being an employee to becoming an entrepreneur?

Step 1

Outcome:
The core category is

Entrepreneurial mind-shifts

Step 2

Outcome:
The main concepts related to the core category are

The types of entrepreneurial mind-shifts, for instance Perception of difficulty Perception of risk, Perception of salaried employment

Step 3

Outcome:
Rough outline of the theoretical model

The main theoretical code is a typology of entrepreneurial mind-shift

Step 4

Outcome:
First written draft of the Theory

Step 5

Outcome:
Enrichment / Modification and integration of the theory in the literature

Step 6

Outcome:
Theory grounded in data

Step 7

In the published version of this study, Step 5 is not presented and Steps 6 and 7 are combined in the presentation of the theory

Figure 5.8 Awakening the dormant dream (Mourmant and Voutsina, 2017)

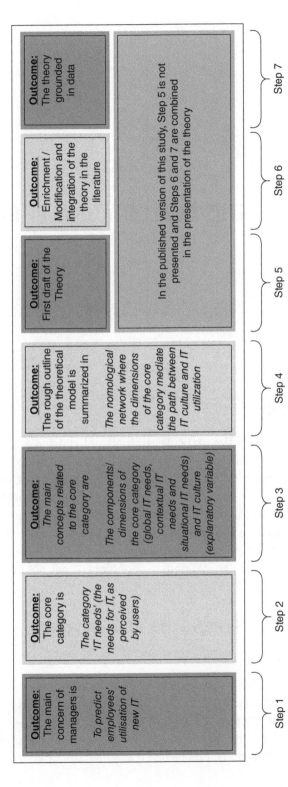

Figure 5.9 A strategic path to study IT use through users' IT culture and IT needs (Walsh, 2014)

6

STRENGTHS AND LIMITATIONS OF GT

'Trust GT, it works! Just do it, use it and publish!' (Glaser, 1998: 254)

INTRODUCTION

In this chapter, we discuss the particular strengths of classic GT as well as its limitations. In doing so, we aim to help you justify the use of the approach as well as recognize and elaborate on its limitations as an approach appropriate to your research project. Here, we discuss GT's particular strengths as its explanatory power, its systematic procedural approach, its discovery potential, and its practical value. We then discuss its limitations as a research approach, focusing on its propositional, not verificational, nature and the confusion induced by so many different GT approaches. We conclude the chapter with a cautionary note that GT may not be for everyone.

THE PARTICULAR STRENGTHS OF A GT APPROACH

Explanatory power

GT's particular strength lies in its potential to offer more than a detailed descriptive account of the subject under study. While many qualitative methodologies will generate rich descriptive accounts of particularistic experiences, they generally fall short of proposing a fully integrated theory that conceptually explains the phenomenon under study, emphasizing a main issue or concern that explains what is really going on in the area under study. While GT does not aim to provide detailed descriptive accuracy, it does illuminate latent patterns of social behavior that explain, rather than describe, behavior that occurs in many diverse groups with a same concern (Glaser, 2003).

As such, it holds particular attraction for management students who are focused on identifying and addressing key management problems. However, many who are new to grounded theory can find it difficult to 'let go' of the rich descriptive detail of qualitative data in service to the explanatory power of abstract conceptual theorizing. It must be stressed that even though some may find that preliminary describing helps them toward conceptualizing, classic GT goes far beyond description to reach explanation and theorizing.

A systematic, full package approach

A decided strength of GT is the methodology's systematic procedures for the abstract conceptualization of latent patterns within a social reality. The decision to use GT is, therefore, a 'full package' decision. It requires the adoption of a systematic set of precise procedures for the collection, analysis, and articulation of a grounded theory. It has been suggested that GT grew in popularity precisely because it proposes systematic procedures, which guarantee some rigor that is often challenged in qualitative studies (Charmaz, 2014b).

You can be assured that following GT's full package approach will result in a conceptual theory. While GT does require that you have the ability to conceptualize and to tolerate ambiguity and even some confusion in enabling the emergence of conceptual insights, GT's delayed-action learning curve means that your skill development increases with every effort. However, generating a grounded theory does take time. Small increments of collecting and coding data allow theoretical ideas to develop and be captured in memos. Thus you must pace yourself, exercising patience and taking whatever time is necessary for the discovery. Rushing or forcing the process might shut down your natural creativity and conceptual ability, exhausting your energy and motivation and leaving your resulting theory thin and incomplete.

At the same time, GT's systematic procedures do not unduly restrict your creative perspective nor your intuitive sense of when to undertake each step in the GT process. The process is iterative with your confidence and competence building with experience. It is perhaps best suited to those who can tolerate, even enjoy, long periods of independent study, analysis, and writing. Indeed, the iterative nature of the methodology frees you to develop your own sense of GT's experiential learning curve and to creatively cycle back and forth through data collection, constant comparative analysis and theoretical sampling until you are satisfied that you have achieved overall theoretical saturation and integration.

Discovery potential

GT has tremendous discovery potential – but this potential is frequently undermined when students ignore the foundational principles of GT – emergence, constant comparison, and theoretical sampling (Glaser, 1978). Staying open to emergent patterns in data offers surprising and exciting theoretical discoveries – what Glaser has termed the 'Eureka' moment (Glaser, 1978: 24).

Some students will claim to employ GT while referring only to their use of constant comparison and theoretical sampling. There is, however, much less clarity around claims to respecting GT's emergent nature. Emergence necessitates that you remain open to what is discovered empirically in the data 'without first having them filtered through and squared with pre-existing hypotheses and biases' (Glaser, 1978: 3) or theoretical frameworks drawn from extant theory. In many qualitative studies, however, emergence is restricted to the analysis phase (e.g. Corley & Gioia, 2004) and with data collection framed through an initial review of the literature (e.g. Partington, 2000). To enable GT's full discovery power, however, a review of the literature is postponed at least until after the core category of the emerging theory has been identified, and preferably until you have drawn a preliminary draft of the emerging theory.

An extensive review of the literature before the emergence of a core category in a GT study is a form of preconception that undermines a basic premise of classic GT, i.e. the theory emerges from the data not from extant theory. While some authors claim that it is close to impossible for any researcher to start research work 'from a blank slate', i.e. without having some prior knowledge of the field, others (e.g. Urquhart & Fernandez, 2013) argue that doing a 'non-committal' literature review *ex ante* helps develop your theoretical sensitivity and a better understanding of the research domain.

While you will commence your work with a general area of research interest, forcing preconceived ideas developed through a previous theoretical framework interferes with GT's discovery power. Instead, getting started in GT means entering the research field with no preconceived problem statement, interview protocols or review of literature but also remaining open to the discovery of a main concern in the area under study and its processing or resolution. Thus, forcing preconceived notions of an initial professional problem or a theoretical framework on the study is suspended in service to seeing what will emerge conceptually by constant comparative analysis.

It is possible that you may have to bend to the wishes of your supervisor in this regard, however, you should discuss the difficulty of conducting a literature review that is relevant to the theory that you will eventually propose *before* the core category has emerged, i.e. without knowing the specific phenomenon you are investigating. Extensive engagement with the literature prior to data collection and analysis runs the risk of thwarting your theoretical sensitivity by clouding your ability to remain open to the emergence of a completely new core category that may not have figured prominently in the literature to date. Practically speaking, preconception may well result in your spending valuable time on an area of literature that proves to be of little significance to the resultant grounded theory. By postponing engagement with the literature at least until the core category has emerged, classic GT treats the literature as just more data to be coded and integrated into the study through constant comparative analysis after the basic conceptual development is well under way, not in advance as is common to other research methodologies. Unless pre-empted by preconception, emergence is natural with the resultant grounded theory often in rupture with existing literature and/or charting new theoretical territory.

Not knowing in the early stages of your study just what will emerge as the core category can create some anxiety and confusion, but rushing or forcing the GT process will undermine your creativity and conceptual abilities, leading to a theory that is thin and incomplete. It can be intimidating to tolerate the uncertainty and subsequent confusion of not knowing in advance and having to remain open to what emerges through the diligent, controlled, and often tedious application of GT's iterative processes of constant comparison and theoretical sampling. Surviving the apparent confusion is important and requires that you take whatever time is necessary and in a manner consistent with your own temporal nature as a student: what Glaser refers to as 'personal pacing' (1998: 49). While this pace may not always align with a supervisor's expectations, you can rely on GT's systematic procedures together with your innate creativity and preconscious processing abilities to foster conceptual ideation and a creativity characterized by the exhilaration that results from sparks of discovery.

Practical value

The motivations for choosing GT are of course varied, but it is worth noting its practical value for many students, particularly for those in the practice of professions, such as management, nursing, medicine, social work, and education. Students speak of this practical value in turning their professional experiences into theories that explain and provide 'access variables' (Glaser & Strauss, 1967: 248-49), enabling more effective interventions and solutions to the problems they may face in their professional practice. In doing so, students not only seek to achieve a contribution to knowledge in their discipline but also to effectively offer a social value through enhanced practice.

LIMITATIONS OF A CLASSIC GROUNDED THEORY APPROACH

GT as propositional, not verificational

Hypothesis testing and verification through the use of statistically valid sets of quantitative data has long been regarded as the gold standard in scientific discovery. This privileging of the positivistic emphasis on theory verification over theory generation has tended to disregard the use of methodologies that may use qualitative data as holding little value, possibly even being unscientific. On the other hand, Morse (1997) also suggests that those trained in qualitative methodologies more traditional than classic GT, and where rich descriptive detail is valued, are theoretically timid and may be too inhibited by what they see to undertake the hard work of conceptualization necessary to produce theory. They may find it hard to 'unlearn' such training, especially if this perspective is reinforced by supervisors and departmental perspectives on what 'good' research entails.

Glaser (2001) suggests that many students simply lack knowledge and competence in conceptualization, and therefore embrace the idea of GT without fully understanding what is required. Charmaz (2014b: 1074) argues, however, that GT has helped to rebalance 'taken-for-granted hierarchies' in academia that try to assert what makes for good research. Indeed, GT's propositional nature reflects the tentative, not factual, nature of all theory; open to modification based on additional data and analysis. Here, GT's particular strength is that it is empirically grounded which therefore adds substance and credibility to its propositional nature.

So many versions of GT

The tendency has been to consider GT a qualitative research approach while ignoring its quantitative roots and its inherent flexibility as a general research methodology that uses any and all types of data (Glaser, 2003, 2005; Holton, 2008). Consequently, we have seen a range of methodologies claiming GT status which, over time, has led to GT being interpreted as synonymous with a more general term, 'grounded theorizing' (Langley, 1999; Locke, 2007) or 'grounded analysis' (Johnson & Harris, 2002: 113). Walsh et al. (2015b: 625) suggest that '[t]his blurring of terms is at the heart of the persistent "rhetorical wrestle" (Glaser, 1998) surrounding grounded theory.'

Despite wide acceptance of methodological pluralism as inevitable and a natural evolution of a methodology (Locke, 2001; Charmaz, 2014a,b; Gibson & Hartman, 2014), Gibson and Hartman (2014: 30) concede that methodological pluralism 'can make the task of understanding what a grounded theory should look like more complicated.' If you are new to research, it is easy to see how you can be easily confused by the multiple versions and the frequent assertion of GT as a qualitative approach, especially if you have been trained in – or are being supervized by someone trained in – the dominant extreme paradigms of positivist quantitative research versus interpretive-constructivist qualitative research. The inevitable consequence is to, often unconsciously, remodel the methodology to suit the dominant genre in your field or to compensate for inadequate GT skill development.

This book is about classic GT as thought-out by Glaser and Strauss (1967) and later elaborated on by Glaser (1978, 1992, 1998, 2001, 2003, 2005, 2007, 2008, 2009, 2011, 2012, 2013, 2014a, 2014b, 2016, 2017). However, beyond being a research approach, GT is fairly close to being a research paradigm in itself. As described in GT's seminal text (Glaser & Strauss, 1967), it is a very broad approach that encompasses endless possibilities to discover significant rupture theories. Glaser and Strauss (1967) provided a general research framework but no precise research guidelines. More precise guidelines were developed subsequently by various authors (Glaser, 1978; Strauss & Corbin, 1998; Corbin & Strauss, 2014; Charmaz, 2006) with different philosophical perspectives (post-positivism, symbolic interactionism, constructivism) that often led them to disagree. This means that the general picture of how to do GT is somewhat blurred. However, we believe that the broadest perspective, open to many possibilities and that allows your creativity to express itself, is that of Glaser perspective as one finds the origins of GT in his doctoral dissertation (Glaser, 1961). Therefore, and as long as you are aware of the debates about the various streams of GT, you should be able to defend your choice of classic GT. You also have to be aware that your dissertation supervisor might not be trained to do GT or if they are, they may have been trained within a different strand of GT.

GT may not be for everyone

GT is not a fit for every student. A GT student requires three characteristics: 'an ability to conceptualize data, an ability to tolerate some confusion, and an ability to tolerate confusion's attendant regression [which are necessary to] ... enable the student to wait for the conceptual sense making to emerge from the data' (Glaser, 2010: 4). You should also be sometimes wary of supervisors who will attempt to 'rescue' you, when you encounter the inevitable confusions of working through a GT study. Many academics who supervize master's students may view GT as a qualitative research methodology and perhaps be skeptical of GT's claims to be a general methodology for research, which may use any type of data, with its own distinct 'full package' set of systematic procedures. Also, your supervisor's subject expertise may risk clouding your ability to remain open to the emergence of a completely new core category that has not figured prominently in the research to date. Practically, it may well result in your being directed to spend valuable time on a literature review in an area that proves to be of little significance to the consequent emergent grounded theory.

The decision to choose classic GT can place you outside the norm in some academic departments and leave you feeling pressured to abandon or compromise GT's full procedures. Attempts to walk the line between classic GT and qualitative 'grounded theorizing' (Holton, 2018) may leave you entrapped in methodologies slurring (Stern, 1994) as you attempt to accommodate standard expectations of qualitative research (e.g. preconceived research question as the focus of the study, extensive initial literature review), while pulling on various qualitative data-collection methods and analysis techniques (e.g. triangulation of data sources, interrater checking, extensive verbatim quoting) and consumed with concerns for what Glaser (2002) has coined 'descriptive capture' (para.9) and ' full coverage' (para. 44) as you proceed to collect large caches of unnecessary, and even sometimes irrelevant, data.

Doing GT does require a certain level of autonomy on your part as you work to find a personal rhythm and fit with the methodology – what Glaser (1978) refers to as 'theoretical pacing.' This experiential aspect of learning GT is highly individual and requires developing a pace that accommodates your temperament as a researcher, the nature of the area under study, and the important cycling through the nonlinear, iterative stages of data collection, coding and memoing, so as to sustain energy and creativity throughout the full theory generation process. Confidence does build as the process progresses, but it takes commitment on your part and confidence on the part of your supervisor to allow GT's delayed action learning process to unfold.

SOME FINAL ADVICE

The decision to use classic GT methodology is a 'full package' decision. It requires the adoption of a systematic set of procedures for the collection, analysis, and articulation of conceptually abstract theory. On the menu of research methodology, classic GT is a 'table d'hôte', not 'à la carte'! You have to take the time to apply all systematic procedures to allow your theory to emerge as grounded in your data. Little increments of collecting and coding allow theoretical ideas to develop into conceptual memos. Significant theoretical realizations come with growth and maturity in the data, and much of this is outside the researcher's conscious awareness until preconscious processing facilitates its conscious emergence (Glaser, 1998: 50). Thus, the researcher must pace themself, exercising patience and accepting nothing until this inevitable emergence has transpired. Surviving the apparent confusion is important, requiring the researcher to take whatever time is necessary for the discovery process, and to take this time in a manner consistent with their own temporal nature as a researcher: what Glaser (1998: 49) refers to as personal pacing. Rushing or forcing the process shuts down the researcher's natural creativity and conceptual ability, exhausting energy and motivation leaving the resultant theory thin and incomplete.

The above advice may seem daunting to you but you should not underestimate the experiential nature of GT's 'full package' methodology and its ability to foster your skill development and confidence. GT does require that you not only have the ability to conceptualize but also the ability to tolerate ambiguity and even some confusion in enabling the emergence of conceptual insights through preconscious processing. That being said, you should not be intimidated as GT's delayed action learning curve means that your skill development increases with each effort made to engage in coding and analyzing data. Continued memo writing in tandem with coding until you achieve saturation on the core category and related concepts will build your memo bank. Throughout the process, each time you experience the pent-up need to sort your memos, do so until eventually you see the overall integration of your theory and are ready to write it up.

This experiential nature of GT cannot be over-emphasized. Once you have gained a level of familiarity with the procedures of conducting a grounded theory study through reading and study of the methodology and, where possible, participation in seminars led by experienced grounded theorists, your skill development can only be advanced through doing. The process is iterative with confidence and competence building with experience. It is perhaps best suited if you can tolerate, even enjoy, long periods of independent study, analysis, and writing.

Of course, skill development is accelerated when you have access to experienced grounded theorists as mentors but many students have produced excellent grounded theories without such mentoring. While reading extensively, yet selectively, regarding the methodological foundations and procedures of GT is important, you should not get caught up in the trap of trying to 'know it all' before stepping into action. As we have already said, confidence and skill grow with practice. Like any new skill, it takes time to develop but GT is highly intuitive. And as Glaser himself says 'Just do it!' and feel the excitement of the 'draw and grab' of GT research.

SUMMARY

In Chapter 6, we discussed the particular strengths of classic GT as its explanatory power, its systematic 'full package' approach, its discovery power, and its practical value for generating theories that are empirically grounded. We also discussed GT's limitations as offering propositional theory, not verification of research results, and the confusion that those new to GT may experience due to the many 'versions' of GT that have emerged over time. We also offered a cautionary note that GT may not be for everyone as it requires the researcher to be able to conceptualize data as well as tolerate the attendant confusion and sense of regression that is necessary for the theory to emerge from data.

GLOSSARY

Analysis techniques The instruments used in a research project to help analyse and make sense of the collected data.

Category A group of people or things that are similar in some way (*Webster* dictionary). In the context of GT and according to Glaser, a category is a 'type of concept, usually used for a higher level of abstraction' (Glaser, 1992: 38).

Coding Classifying data into categories.

Concept An abstract or generic idea generalized from particular instances (*Webster* dictionary).

Conceptualization Naming a pattern found in data.

Constant comparison Comparing constantly all data, as they are collected.

Core category The category that appears to explain the most significantly how the main concern is processed, managed, and/or resolved.

Data-collection method Medium through which data are collected.

Dimension A measurable component of a concept or category. Dimensions are not interchangeable; they are complementary to define a concept or category.

Emergence No preconception. The theory emerges from the data.

Formal grounded theory A grounded theory developed at a higher level of empirical generalization and/or conceptual abstraction by extending the general implications of the core category of a substantive grounded theory through subsequent theoretical sampling across a wide range of settings and/or disciplines.

Framework The general set of guidelines proposed by some authors that a researcher might choose to follow in a given project.

Incident   'Something dependent on or subordinate to' the phenomenon that is being investigated, an 'occurrence' (*Webster* dictionary) of something that emerges from the data and strikes the researcher as being remarkable and noteworthy.

Interchangeable indicators   Empirical incidents in data that are interchangeable in indicating a concept (i.e. indicating the same concept) but which may also bring out different properties or values of the conceptual idea to enhance theory elaboration.

Main concern   Prime motivator, interest, or problem investigated.

Memos   Notes written about the data and the connections/relationships between categories are written throughout the constant comparative process. The researcher captures her emerging ideas through the writing of memos.

Memoing   Writing ideas as they emerge.

Metaphor   A figure of speech in which a word or phrase literally denoting one kind of object or idea is used in place of another to suggest a likeness or analogy between them (*Webster* dictionary).

Methodology   The specific combination of research data-collection methods and analysis techniques used in a research project.

Open coding   Initial coding stage in classic GT to identify the main concern and core category.

Paradigm   The researcher's world view.

Pattern   A discernible coherent system based on the intended interrelationship of component parts (*Webster* dictionary); A regular and intelligible form or sequence discernible in the way in which something happens or is done (*Oxford* dictionary).

Preconceptions/Conceptual pollution   Influence from existing concepts not grounded in the data.

Preconscious processing/Conceptual leap   Creative and seemingly serendipitous insights.

Property   A characteristic of a concept or category.

Saturation   When in coding and analyzing data, no new concepts or properties emerge.

Selective coding   Coding around the core category.

Substantive   Having substance – involving matters of major or practical importance to all concerned (*Webster* dictionary).

Substantive coding   The process of conceptualizing the empirical data in which the theory is grounded. Incidents in the empirical data are coded for indicators of concepts from which a grounded theory is then generated. Substantive coding consists of both the initial open coding of data and the selective coding of data once the core category has emerged.

Substantive grounded theory   A grounded theory developed within a specific setting and context and generalizable to a limited number of similar settings or groups.

Theoretical coding   Coding that conceptualizes and models relationships between concepts.

Theoretical sampling   Process through which data are selected and collected while guided by the emerging theory.

Theoretical saturation   When further data yield no new concepts or additional elaboration of their properties and dimensions.

Theoretical sensitivity   The capacity to conceptualize and formulate a theory as it emerges from data.

Theoretical sorting   Sorting of memos to support conceptualization.

REFERENCES

Baskerville, R. and Pries-Heje, J. (1999) Grounded action research: a method for understanding IT in practice, *Accounting, Management and Information Technology, 9*(1): 1-23.

Bhaskar, R. (1975) *A Realist Theory of Science*. Brighton, UK: Harvester.

Bhaskar, R. (2002) *Reflections on Meta-Reality: A Philosophy for the Present*. New Delhi: Sage Publications.

Bryant, A. and Charmaz, K. (eds) (2007) *The Sage Handbook of Grounded Theory*. London: Sage Publications.

Bryman, A. (1998) 'Quantitative and Qualitative Research Strategies in Knowing the Social World', in T. May and M. Williams (eds), *Knowing the Social World*, pp. 138-57. Buckingham: Open University Press.

Cartwright, N. (2003) *Causation: One Word, Many Things*. London: Centre for Philosophy of Natural and Social Science.

Charmaz, K. (2006) *Constructing Grounded Theory: A Practical Guide through Qualitative Analysis*. London: Sage Publications.

Charmaz, K. (2014a) *Constructing Grounded Theory* (2nd edn). Thousand Oaks, CA: Sage Publications.

Charmaz, K. (2014b) Grounded theory in global perspective: reviews by international researchers, *Qualitative Inquiry, 20*(9): 1074-84.

Connelly, C.E., Zweig, D., Webster, J. and Trougakos, J.P. (2012) Knowledge hiding in organizations, *Journal of Organizational Behavior, 33*(1): 64-88.

Corbin, J. and Strauss, A.L. (2014) *Basics of Qualitative Research: Techniques and Procedures for Developing Grounded Theory* (4th edn). London: Sage Publications.

Corley, K.G. and Gioia, D.A. (2004) Identity ambiguity and change in the wake of a corporate spin-off, *Administrative Science Quarterly, 49*(2):173-208.

Eisenhardt, K.M. (1989) Building theories from case study research, *Academy of Management Review, 14*(4): 532-50.

Gibson, B. and Hartman, J. (2014) *Rediscovering Grounded Theory*. London: Sage Publications.

Glaser, B.G. (1961) 'Some functions of recognition in a research organization', unpublished doctoral dissertation, Columbia University, New York.

Glaser, B.G. (1965) The constant comparative method of qualitative analysis, *Social Problems, 12*: 436–45.

Glaser, B.G. (1978) *Theoretical Sensitivity: Advances in the Methodology of Grounded Theory*. Mill Valley, CA: Sociology Press.

Glaser, B.G. (1992) *Basics of Grounded Theory Analysis*. Mill Valley, CA: Sociology Press.

Glaser, B.G. (1995) *Grounded Theory: 1984–1994*. Mill Valley, CA: Sociology Press.

Glaser, B.G. (1998) *Doing Grounded Theory: Issues and Discussions*. Mill Valley, CA: Sociology Press.

Glaser, B.G. (2001) *The Grounded Theory Perspective: Conceptualization Contrasted With Description*. Mill Valley, CA: Sociology Press.

Glaser, B.G. (2002) Constructivist grounded theory?, *Forum: Qualitative Sozial forschung/ Forum: Qualitative Social Research, 3*(3). Available at www.qualitative-research.net/index.php/fqs/article/view/825/1792 (accessed 6 March 2016).

Glaser, B.G. (2003) *The Grounded Theory Perspective II: Description's Remodeling of Grounded Theory Methodology*. Mill Valley, CA: Sociology Press.

Glaser, B.G. (2005) *The Grounded Theory Perspective III: Theoretical Coding*. Mill Valley, CA: Sociology Press.

Glaser, B.G. (2007) *Doing Formal Grounded Theory*. Mill Valley, CA: Sociology Press.

Glaser, B.G. (2008) *Doing Quantitative Grounded Theory*. Mill Valley, CA: Sociology Press.

Glaser, B.G. (2009) *Jargonizing: Using the Grounded Theory Vocabulary*. Mill Valley, CA: Sociology Press.

Glaser, B. G. (2010). The future of grounded theory. *Grounded Theory Review, 9*(2), 1–14.

Glaser, B.G. (2011) *Getting Out of the Data: Grounded Theory Conceptualization*. Mill Valley, CA: Sociology Press.

Glaser, B.G. (2012) *Stop, Write: Writing Grounded Theory*. Mill Valley, CA: Sociology Press.

Glaser, B.G. (2013) *No Preconceptions: The Grounded Theory Dictum*. Mill Valley, CA: Sociology Press.

Glaser, B.G. (2014a) *Applying Grounded Theory: A Neglected Option*. Mill Valley, CA: Sociology Press.

Glaser, B.G. (2014b) *Memoing: A Vital Grounded Theory Procedure*. Mill Valley, CA: Sociology Press.

Glaser, B.G. (2016) *The Cry for Help: Preserving Autonomy Doing GT Research*. Mill Valley, CA: Sociology Press.

Glaser, B.G. (2017) *Grounded Descriptions: A No No*. Mill Valley, CA: Sociology Press.

Glaser, B.G. and Strauss, A.L. (1965) *Awareness of Dying*. Chicago, IL: Aldine.

Glaser, B.G. and Strauss, A.L. (1967) *The Discovery of Grounded Theory: Strategies for Qualitative Research*. New York: Aldine.

Glaser, B.G. and Strauss, A.L. (1971) *Status Passage: A Formal Theory*. Mill Valley, CA: Sociology Press.

Gregor, S. (2006) The nature of theory in information systems, *MIS Quarterly*, *30*(3): 611–42.

Holton, J.A. (2007) Rehumanising knowledge work through fluctuating support networks: a grounded theory study, *The Grounded Theory Review*, *6*(2): 23–46.

Holton, J.A. (2008) Grounded theory as a general research methodology, *The Grounded Theory Review*, *7*(2): 67–89.

Holton, J.A. (2018) 'From Grounded Theory and Grounded Theorizing in Qualitative Research', in C. Cassell, A. Cunliffe and G. Grandy (eds), *The SAGE Handbook of Qualitative Business and Management Research Methods*, pp. 233–50. London: Sage Publications.

Holton, J.A. and Walsh, I. (2017) *Fundamentals of Classic Grounded Theory: Applications with Qualitative and Quantitative Data*. Thousand Oaks, CA: Sage Publications.

Johnson, P. and Harris, D. (2002) 'Qualitative and Quantitative Issues in Research Design', in D. Partington (ed.), *Essential Skills for Management Research*, pp. 99–135. London: Sage Publications.

Johnson, R. and Onwuegbuzie, A.J. (2004) Mixed methods research: a research paradigm whose time has come, *Educational Researcher*, *33*(14): 14–26.

Langley, A. (1999) Strategies for theorizing from process data, *Academy of Management Review*, *24*(4): 691–710.

Lazarsfeld, P.F. and Henry, N.W. (1968) *Latent Structure Analysis*. Boston, MA: Houghton Mifflin.

Locke, K. (2001) *Grounded Theory in Management Research*. London: Sage Publications.

Locke, K. (2007) 'Rational Control and Irrational Free-Play: Dual-Thinking Modes as Necessary Tension in Grounded Theorizing', in A. Bryant and K. Charmaz (eds), *The SAGE Handbook of Grounded Theory*, pp. 565–79. London: Sage Publications.

Lohse, H. (2018) 'Managers engaging in professional doctoral studies in business and management: motivational drivers, facilitators and barriers', unpublished DBA dissertation.

Loyola de Oliveira, L. (work in progress) 'Quality in higher education: from perceptions to construction', unpublished PhD dissertation.

Miles, M.B. and Huberman, A.M. (1994) *Qualitative Data Analysis: An Expanded Sourcebook* (2nd edn). Thousand Oaks, CA: Sage Publications.

Morse, J.M. (ed.) (1997) *Completing a Qualitative Research Project: Details and Dialogue*. Thousand Oaks, CA: Sage Publications.

Mourmant, G., Gallivan, M.J. and Kalika, M. (2009) Another road to IT turnover: the entrepreneurial path, *European Journal of Information Systems, 18*(5): 498-521.

Mourmant, G. and Voutsina, K. (2010) 'From IT Employee to IT Entrepreneur: the Concept of IT Entrepreneurial Epiphany', *ICIS 2010 Proceedings*, Paper 208. Available at https://aisel.aisnet.org/icis2010_submissions/208

Mourmant, G. and Voutsina, K. (2017) Awakening the dormant dream: the concept of entrepreneurial mind-shifts, *ACM SIGMIS Database: The DATABASE for Advances in Information Systems, 48*(3): 110-37.

Nandram, S.S., Mourmant, G., Norlyk Smith, E., Heaton, D.P. and Bindlish, P.K. (2018) Understanding entrepreneurial decision-making by objectivizing subtle cues, *Journal of Management, Spirituality & Religion, 15*(5): 398-423.

Partington, D. (2000) Building grounded theories of management action, *British Journal of Management, 11*(2): 91-102.

Peirce, C.S. (1965) 'The First Rule of Reason', in *Collected Papers of Charles Peirce*. Cambridge, MA: Belknap.

Peng, A.C., Schaubroeck, J.M. and Li, Y. (2014) Social exchange implications of own and coworkers' experiences of supervisory abuse, *Academy of Management Journal, 57*(5): 1385-1405.

Schmidkontz, M. (2017) *'Plaisir au travail en Business Schools françaises'*, unpublished DBA dissertation.

Simmons, O.E. (2010) 'Is that a real theory or did you just make it up?': Teaching classic grounded theory, *The Grounded Theory Review, 9*(2): 15-38.

Smith, M. (2010) Testable theory development for small-N studies: critical realism and middle-range theory, *International Journal of Information Technology and Systems Approach, 3*(1): 41-56.

Stern, P.N. (1994) 'Eroding Grounded Theory', in J.M. Morse (ed.), *Critical Issues in Qualitative Research Methods*, pp. 212-23. Thousand Oaks, CA: Sage Publications.

Strauss, A.L. and Corbin, J.M. (1998) *Basics of qualitative research techniques*. Thousand Oaks, CA: Sage publications.

Tiers, G., Mourmant, G. and Leclercq-Vandelannoitte, A. (2013) L'envol vers le Cloud: un phénomène de maturations multiples, *Systèmes d'information & management, 18*(4): 7-42.

Urquhart, C. and Fernandez, W. (2013) Using grounded theory method in information systems: the researcher as blank slate and other myths, *Journal of Information Technology, 28*(3): 224-36.

Vazeux, A. (2018) *'Les clés permettant d'assurer le succès d'une entreprise dans le secteur de la restauration "fast casual" en France'*, unpublished master's thesis.

Walsh, I. (2014) A strategic path to study IT use through users' IT culture and IT needs: a mixed-method grounded theory, *Journal of Strategic Information Systems*, *23*(2): 146-73.

Walsh, I. (2015a) Using quantitative data in mixed-design grounded theory studies: an enhanced path to formal grounded theory in information systems, *European Journal of Information Systems, 24*(5): 531-57.

Walsh, I. (2015b) '*Comment Transformer une Experience Pratique en Théorie: Auti-ethnographie et Théorie Enracinée*', in P. Beaulieuand M. Kalika (eds), *La Création de Connaissance par les Managers*. Éditions EMS, www.editions-ems.fr/.

Walsh, I., Holton, J.A., Bailyn, L., Fernandez, W., Levina, N. and Glaser, B. (2015a) What grounded theory is ... a critically reflective conversation among scholars, *Organizational Research Methods, 18*(4): 581-99.

Walsh, I., Holton, J.A., Bailyn, L., Fernandez, W., Levina, N. and Glaser, B. (2015b) Moving the management field forward, *Organizational Research Methods, 18*(4): 620-28.

Walsh, I., Kefi, H., and Baskerville, R. (2010) Managing culture creep: toward a strategic model of user IT culture, *Journal of Strategic Information Systems*, *19*(4): 257-80.

INDEX

Fold a Giraffe

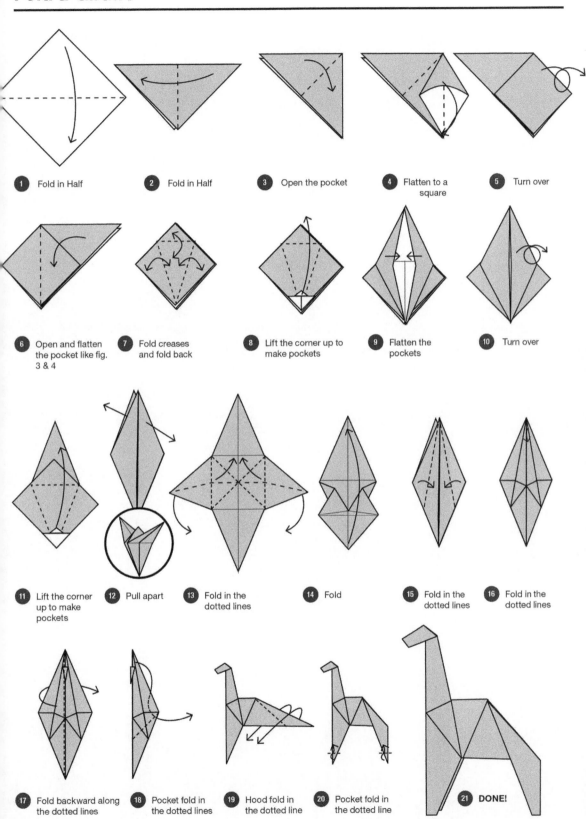

1. Fold in Half
2. Fold in Half
3. Open the pocket
4. Flatten to a square
5. Turn over
6. Open and flatten the pocket like fig. 3 & 4
7. Fold creases and fold back
8. Lift the corner up to make pockets
9. Flatten the pockets
10. Turn over
11. Lift the corner up to make pockets
12. Pull apart
13. Fold in the dotted lines
14. Fold
15. Fold in the dotted lines
16. Fold in the dotted lines
17. Fold backward along the dotted lines
18. Pocket fold in the dotted lines
19. Hood fold in the dotted line
20. Pocket fold in the dotted line
21. DONE!